AF691542

Philip Hyland has been practising employment law since 1992 and since 2002 in his own boutique employment law firm PJH Law. He is well versed in the law and practice of managing redundancy situations, advising employers for over 30 years on all aspects of redundancy from large scale site closures through to discrete departmental re-organisations. He has appeared as representative at hundreds of Employment Tribunal hearings, a good proportion of which were on claims related to redundancy including: unfair selection, discriminatory selection, redundancy payments and collective consultation. At least two of his redundancy cases have ended up as published precedents.

Collette Moore recently joined PJH Law as a newly qualified solicitor working alongside Philip Hyland. Collette's interest in employment law began several years ago whilst on placement in America during her undergraduate law degree. Her dedication to the area continued throughout her studies on the Legal Practice Course and Masters in Law. This, coupled with several years of practical experience in the legal profession, positions her as a valuable asset and promising contributor to the firm's expertise in employment law.

A Practical Guide to Redundancy

Second Edition

A Practical Guide to Redundancy

Second Edition

Philip Hyland

BA, MA, FRSA

Solicitor

Collette Moore

LLB, LLM

Solicitor

Law Brief Publishing

Published 2024 by Law Brief Publishing, an imprint of Law Brief Publishing Ltd
30 The Parks
Minehead
Somerset
TA24 8BT

www.lawbriefpublishing.com

Paperback: 978-1-916698-29-1

PREFACE

Aimed at HR Managers and Employment Law practitioners, this book provides readers with an overview of the law underpinning redundancy dismissals, as well as practical guidance on managing the redundancy process. It gives practical assistance in meeting your organisation's aims of reducing the number of employees, whilst minimising the risk of a successful challenge.

In short, this book will give you tips and tactics to ensure successful outcomes.

The law stated in this book is believed to be up to date on the 25th January 2024.

Thank you to the team at Law Brief Publishing and the team at PJH Law, Solicitors for their assistance in the writing, editing and publishing process.

Thank you also to all my clients and in particular Les Williams, Rod Graham, Allison Long, Kevin Taylor and John Mockler, who I have learnt an immense amount from.

Philip Hyland
January 2024

CONTENTS

INTRODUCTION

My name is Philip Hyland. I have been practising employment law since 1992.

What led me into employment law?

Long story but let's cut to the chase to noon one afternoon in mid-December 1983.

I came home from Orpington Sixth Form College, where I was studying A levels, to find my Dad in the house in tears.

That morning my Dad had been made redundant. He had been met by his manager and a personnel manager that morning, out of the blue, given 12 weeks notice of termination of employment, an outline of his redundancy payment and sent home.

My Dad had been with his employer since the age of 16. He was 49. He never secured another permanent employed position again. He took a much reduced pension aged 50.

Since then my Dad has always said that big companies expect loyalty but don't show their staff loyalty. He might have a point. For a long time he felt bitter about the way he was treated.

My Dad's redundancy cloud was silver lined for me.

Firstly, as I was at an age where I was deciding what I wanted to do, the unfair treatment meted out to Dad meant I focussed my sights on Law.

As I saw a university course as a bet on my future, I hedged my course choice. I put Law and Politics down on my UCAS form.

Dad's lack of job meant my grant application was means tested. I received a full maintenance grant whilst I studied free of tuition fees at Hull University. Blackadder fans will know that Hull is one of the top three UK universities alongside Oxford and Cambridge.

For younger readers, a full maintenance grant is what the local council paid you to attend university and covered your living expenses.

This early experience of the harsh treatment sometimes meted out by employers when needing to reduce costs during a recession led me into specialising in employment law.

What I hadn't realised when I made my course choice, but I know now, is the strong link between employment law and politics.

An experience on the threshold of adulthood led me into becoming an employment law solicitor.

Why is this book necessary?

It's necessary because redundancy is a fact of working life, increasingly so. Like income tax and death, redundancy is inevitable.

There are two key drivers of redundancy: technological progress and the economy.

This introduction is being written on a laptop keyboard, not a typewriter. Typewriters, along with workers employed by typewriter businesses, have become obsolete.

If a society wants progress, jobs become redundant as collateral damage to that march of progress. Redundancy is baked into our way of life – whether it is upgrading to the next iteration of iPhone or taking an Uber instead of a taxi. Creative destruction leaves a trail of job casualties in its wake.

Looking over the Hyland family history we have, within the last century, family members whose occupations are listed as "glass blower" and "journeyman." The remorseless progress of technology has left a scorch mark on those jobs which no longer exist in any recognisable quantity in the UK. The job title "journeyman" is applied to hardworking but technically limited footballers ploughing their furrow in the lower leagues.

When I first started work at Hull City Council in the 1980s, a long serving employee who had started work there in the 1950s told me that part of his job in the early 1950s was to light the fires in the office fireplaces, during Winter.

With the advent of modern boilers that employee had found a more productive use of his time.

Productivity is key. If it takes less resource to create a product or service, the cost of that product or service should fall.

With the much trailed advent of artificial intelligence and robotics, a changing and transformed workplace is inevitable.

Many professions requiring brain power rather than brawn will be affected.

No doubt an algorithm will be developed to write law books.

An artificially intelligent robot will be promulgating Employment Tribunal judgments (some might say they are doing so already in the cash strapped Ministry of Justice!).

It is always unwise to try to predict the future when it comes to technology. For example, who would have said in the year 2000 that by 2024 manual car handwashes would have overtaken automated car washes in the U.K. and application ChatGPT could churn out full length books?

Subject to some counter-examples, the trend in technology is clear. Whilst some sectors may regress (car washes), most sectors are deploying technology in a structured and systematic way, impacting jobs.

Starting in employment law in 1992 my career has not only seen the impact that technology can have on the workplace but also the economic cycle. Recessions and booms, despite some politicians' promises to abolish them, are ever-present.

The early 1990s saw a huge recession with interest rates reaching 15%, the pound dropping out of the European Exchange Rate Mechanism, and an almighty property crash.

That recession affected all occupations. The Job Centre at which I signed on had architects, accountants, lawyers, plumbers, and brickies joining me in the queue.

Those with mobile skills went to work abroad in the European free market. Epitomising the hard times, once prosperous Bradley Stoke in Bristol was nicknamed Sadly Broke.

The Great Financial Crash of 2007/2008 likewise took a scythe to the economy, with sectors like financial services, construction, and the residential property market having to shrink.

Predicting recessions, like predicting technological advances, is a fools' game. Safe to say that recessions are reasonably regular in the UK and whilst we can't predict when a recession will happen, it will usually follow a period of economic growth when the economy overheats.

What sort of book will it be?

In short, this book will be both readable and practical.

A book that adds value by minimising the risk of incurring your employer liability through a poorly handled redundancy exercise.

That liability could either be a legal one measured in pounds and pence or a reputational one measured in disaffected former employees or poor morale amongst remaining employees.

Both liabilities need to be avoided.

Besides a needy desire to leave an employment law legacy other than some occasionally cited law cases, I wanted to help and guide those with less experience than me through the difficult terrain of making redundancies. The book is a legacy, of sorts, but hopefully a practical and helpful one.

I have 30 years' experience of having a front row seat watching the East Midlands economy ebb and flow like an unpredictable tidal pattern.

A redundancy wave is coming, we just can't set our clock by it and we need to know what to do when it hits.

Year after year the same mistakes are made. One of my stock sayings is that there are ten different plots in employment law cases, the only thing that changes is the actors playing the parts.

Whilst some HR practitioners have spent a long time sharpening the redundancy saw and can make job cuts with the minimum of effort, many practitioners do not have first-hand redundancy experience and because of that lack of experience and know how the same fundamental errors are made year in and year out.

Whilst there are plenty of books out there reciting employment law, chapter and verse, there are very few, if any, guiding the reader into putting the rubber of employment law knowledge onto the tarmac of the workplace road.

Who is the book aimed at?

This book is aimed at HR professionals. It is also aimed at newly qualified legal advisers.

What are the book's objectives, the KPIs?

The aims of the book are fourfold:

i. It is to give the HR Practitioner a solid underpinning and stable foundations in the law related to making redundancies.

   HR Practitioners need to have the underpinning knowledge to support their actions and advice.

   What I will not give the reader though is a turgid recital of either the statute law or case law. Case law and statute law will only be referred to if absolutely necessary.

   You will come away with the key pieces of employment law, as well as the contextual background to know where those pieces fit in the redundancy jigsaw.

ii. The intention is to give practical guidance and know how on putting the law into practice, in particular to leave the employee feeling that they have been fairly treated and the practitioner feeling they have done a good job.

   A good job in practitioner terms is having no liability following an exercise that is fraught with financial risk.

Over the last 30 years I have advised on many large scale, small scale, and mid-scale redundancies. I have seen first-hand how skilled Practitioners go about making redundancies.

Some employer clients have been in sectoral decline and have had to manage that decline by reducing their headcount slowly but surely over the years.

HR Practitioners in those sectors, through practice, have become skilled at headcount reductions. Their redundancy saw is sharp and can cut through the most difficult scenario.

The very best HR Practitioners come out of a redundancy exercise with their reputation not only intact but enhanced, gaining respect from those who are left in the business but also from those who have been made redundant.

Larger redundancy exercises are sometimes a joint effort with the trade unions or employee forums playing a key part in ensuring the redundancy plans and proposals are fit for purpose, prior to implementation.

Over the years I have witnessed much best practice as well as many basic errors. This book aims to get over that best practice in a reader friendly and practical way to ensure that basic errors are kept to an absolute minimum, if not avoided completely.

iii. I will share behavioural insights gained from 30 years of advising on redundancy. Employees react to the situation they are in.

Employers play a large part in how the redundancy situation is communicated and framed to employees who are at risk of redundancy.

At risk employees can react positively to a redundancy situation or negatively – framing a redundancy situation to elicit a positive response is possible.

Examples of what draws a positive response will be given in this book. The objective for any employer should be to make redundancy as positive an experience as possible.

Many employees I have advised over the years have said that redundancy was the best thing to have happened to them.

With regard to behavioural insights it is by and large received wisdom that those employers who push decisions down to employees and allow them autonomy to act and make their own decisions are the employers that have harmonious and productive workplaces.

The GM plant in Fremont California went from being the worst car plant in the US to the best in the US within the space of three years purely by instilling a lean manufacturing ethic into the workplace. Integral to lean processes is ensuring that employees are empowered to make their own decisions. That insight about empowerment has relevancy in a redundancy situation.

Employment Law at its core is regulation of how an employer treats its employees. Employers who display commitment to their employees and treat them fairly are also shown to be the businesses that do best.

iv. Making a redundancy is a process. A process is a left sided brain activity. The best practitioners engage the right side of their brain, the empathetic side, to ensure that their employees feel as though they have been fairly treated during the process.

As practitioners will know through psychometric testing of their employees and prospective employees the brain is two sided. Broadly the right brain is empathetic, implicit, intuitive and contextual, the left side is detail and task orientated.

The book will shift from the right side of the brain to the left.

Achieving a harmonious redundancy exercise is ensuring a balance between the left and right brain output. Use the right brain to see the big picture, the context, the employee's point of view and the left brain to put a detailed plan into practice which respects and observes both the employees' rights and their self-respect.

When looking at the substantive law, a left side brain activity, I will provide relevant context to the law so that practitioners will know how the law fits into the overall sweep of workplace regulation. Standing back and looking at the context is a right sided activity.

When looking at putting the law into practice I will stand back and look at an overall helicopter view of the process, a right brain activity, as well as getting down into the weeds and looking at the process in detail, a left sided brain activity.

I will also look at the best way of putting the law into practice that minimises the risk of the employee feeling poorly treated, a right brain, empathetic activity.

By the end of the book practitioners will have a good grasp of the key tenets of redundancy law and where those tenets fall within the grand sweep of employment law.

On finishing the book practitioners will feel confident about formulating a plan to make redundancies as well as putting that plan into practice causing the minimum upset to employees.

Let me know how you get on with both the book and any learnings you have put into practice. Email me at philip@pjhlaw.co.uk.

CHAPTER ONE

SURVEYING THE TERRAIN

Let's stand back and see where the law relating to redundancy in the workplace has sprung from and when.

Before we look at that context, when making any redundancies, there are five key employee rights. These are:

1. Contractual rights.
2. Statutory Rights: Redundancy Payments.
3. Statutory Rights: Employment Rights Act and the Right not to be Unfairly Dismissed.
4. Statutory Rights: Right to have collective representation and negotiation.
5. Statutory Rights: Right not to be Discriminated against.

Contractual Rights

I was born in 1965. Statutory employment rights have been around all of my life.

Statutory employment rights have not been around for all of my parents' lives. My parents were born in 1933 and 1934 respectively.

Whilst technological advances and economic cycles have been with us since well before Jethro Tull invented his seed drill back in 1701 and tulips became an investment fad, the law relating to the impact of a changing workplace has only really developed since the 1960s.

Prior to the 1960s rights in the workplace were mainly governed by the contract. There was the rather patriarchal, upstairs downstairs, Downton Abbey-esque concept of Master and Servant.

Up until the 1960s, there was a free market for labour. But the market was lightly regulated. The only key rights employees had when their employer deemed the employee surplus to requirements, or redundant in modern parlance, were contractual ones. The employers wrote and write the contract.

The key contractual right on termination was to notice. Within the contract employees will have a term governing how much notice in terms of weeks or months their employer must give to terminate the contract.

One of the key payments in a redundancy exercise is a payment in lieu of notice or payment for a notice period.

Other contractual rights can include enhanced redundancy payments.

Statutory Rights: Redundancy Payments

The 1960s saw a sea change. Not only did Bob Dylan go electric, but it was recognised that to compete the UK economy needed to re-structure. Politicians saw that re-structuring would be painful and that employees had few rights.

Parliament acted to reduce the pain to employees by giving them workplace rights to minimise the impact of the economic re-structuring.

Recognising that "the white heat of technology" would leave scorch marks on inefficient and over-resourced sectors of the economy, Harold

Wilson, the prime minister, passed the Redundancy Payments Act 1965 onto the statute books.

The Redundancy Payments Act 1965 [RPA] gave a method of calculation for redundancy payments as well as definitions for what amounted to a redundancy situation.

Those definitions and methodologies have largely survived.

The original sections of the RPA dealing with definitions and calculations for redundancy payments have been transposed into later legislation, currently the Employment Rights Act 1996.

Some provisions of the RPA have not survived the march of progress and have been made redundant as changing attitudes make them obsolete.

For example, under the 1965 Act women were not entitled to a redundancy payment if they were dismissed as redundant after the age of 60, the age for men being 65.

The age limits have themselves been made redundant. Now any employee, however old, will be entitled to a redundancy payment if they meet the qualifying conditions.

Employers were originally reimbursed the cost of a redundancy payment by central government to encourage employers to become more productive by shedding unproductive employees. The RPA was not only a way of giving employees a soft landing if they lost their job, the re-imbursement provisions actually incentivised employers to bite the re-structuring bullet.

The right to employer reimbursement disappeared after 1979.

The right to a redundancy payment is a cornerstone right for UK employees. The law is well established, reasonably well understood, and there are very few disputes about an employee's entitlement to a statutory redundancy payment.

Statutory Rights: Unfair Dismissal

1971 saw the Industrial Relations Act come into force which introduced the concept of unfair dismissal.

The right not to be unfairly dismissed is the second cornerstone right for UK employees.

Redundancy is a potentially fair reason for dismissal.

Despite the law on unfair redundancy dismissal being relatively static, claims for redundancy unfair dismissal are still widespread.

Practitioners may be cutting corners, acting in ignorance or making mistakes, leaving many employees to bring claims for unfair dismissal arising out of their redundancy dismissal.

Leaving aside the time and cost involved in defending a claim, there is also reputational risk both within and without the organisation if you are seen not to treat employees fairly.

Statutory Rights: Discrimination

The mid-1970s saw the UK joining the European Economic Community, the EEC, later known as the EU.

Joining the EEC meant the UK had to abide by the rules of the club which are set out in the founding treaty, the Treaty of Rome.

One of the key rules of the club is that member states have to implement EU rules, known as directives, within 2 years of those rules being passed by the European Parliament.

Some of those rules have dynamic effect. One of the rules was that the UK could not have any law in place which treated men and women in a discriminatory way.

It took until the mid-1990s for the law to recognise that the requirement under the redundancy payment legislation was discriminatory. Part time employees defined as those who work fewer than 16 hours per week on average had to have five years service compared to full time workers who only had to have two.

Based on workforce surveys, it was found that far more women than men worked part time and the differing service requirements were indirectly discriminatory. Those requirements were removed.

In the 1970s the Race Relations Act and the Sex Discrimination Act passed into law.

Pretty much all of the discrimination law has been consolidated into one statute, the Equality Act 2010.

Practitioners have to be alive to discrimination and bias intruding into their decision-making process during a redundancy exercise.

The right not to be discriminated against for having a protected characteristic is the third cornerstone right.

The protected characteristics are:

1. Age.

2. Disability.

3. Gender reassignment.

4. Marriage and civil partnership.

5. Pregnancy and maternity.

6. Race.

7. Religion or belief.

8. Sex.

9. Sexual orientation.

That's right readers, discrimination law covers everybody. We all have at least 3 of those protected characteristics each.

There are a number of different types of discrimination employees and workers are protected from and have the right not to suffer.

The key concept is that discrimination is "prohibited conduct." Conduct prohibited under discrimination law includes:

i) Direct discrimination – treating an employee or worker less favourably because of a protected characteristic. In redundancy that means discriminating against an employee by selecting him or her for redundancy because of a protected characteristic.

ii) Indirect discrimination – applying a practice, provision or criterion that adversely impacts employees with a particular protected characteristic. Possible prohibited conduct could be part time employees in the pool being selected ahead of full-time employees, or older employees being selected ahead of younger employees.

iii) Duty to make reasonable adjustments for employees and workers with disabilities to ensure that a criterion, provision or practice does not put an employee or worker at a substantial disadvantage. Adjustments could be made to the pool or in determining who is offered alternative employment that is available.

iv) The requirement for an employer not to treat an employee or worker less favourably because of something arising in consequence of a disability. Typically, this means disregarding disability related absence when scoring an employee for redundancy.

v) Harassment is subjecting an employee or worker to unwanted conduct that has the purpose or effect of creating an intimidating, hostile, degrading, or offensive environment for the employee or worker. Harassment can come into play during a redundancy exercise. For example, a female employee may reject her line manager's sexual advances, that line manager allows that rejection to taint his scoring of that employee during a redundancy exercise.

vi) Victimisation is treating an employee or worker less favourably because the employee or worker has committed a protected act. Protected acts are:

   a. Bringing a claim under the Equality Act 2010. That is self-explanatory. If an employee is suing their employer for discrimination, the employer cannot pick on the employee during a redundancy exercise.

   b. Giving evidence in a claim under the Equality Act 2010. Again self-explanatory as (a).

   c. Doing any other thing for the purposes of or in connection with the Equality Act 2010. That's a pretty big catch all but will cover grievances about discrimination, even if they are not couched formally as contraventions of the Equality Act 2010.

   d. Making an allegation (whether or not express) that the employer or an employee has breached the Equality Act 2010. As above at (c).

Those paying attention will notice that the right not to be discriminated against covers more than just employees, it covers agency workers as well as workers, typically consultants who are engaged by the employer.

Discrimination is a very live issue in the workplace and in society. The evidence shows that there are glass ceilings, that certain sections of society are not reflected and represented at the higher echelons of organisation's management.

In 2022 of all the FTSE 250 companies, just 4.8% were held by women. 6% of FTSE one hundred business have no board member who is from a BAME background.

Law firms and the judiciary are not the most diverse organisations.

As financial risks, unfair dismissal has a compensatory award capped at a year's salary or around £105,707.00, whichever is the lower.

Discrimination claims have uncapped compensatory awards. Successful Claimants could be awarded 6 or 7 figure awards, if a Claimant has lost a job through discrimination and has then suffered substantial losses.

Practitioners should keep an eagle eye out for potential discrimination issues. Often decisions about employment or continued employment is taken at a sub-conscious level. Line managers appoint or retain in their likeness, thereby reinforcing existing structures. One key case in Equality Law is King v Great Britain China Centre [1992] ICR 516 where Neill LJ astutely observed that discrimination was often based on an assumption that someone "would not fit in," and that evidence of discrimination was not always available as "discriminators rarely admit discrimination, even to themselves."

The law on discrimination has developed over the years. In particular the law recognises that discrimination exists but evidence of discrimination may not always exist in a tangible and clear way.

The days where landlords could advertise a vacant property with a sign saying "No dogs, blacks or Irish" are thankfully long gone. Whilst the signs may have gone, the thought processes behind the signs are still present in a minority of people.

The law therefore can draw inferences that discrimination has taken place. An inference can be drawn where there is less favourable treatment, a difference in protected characteristic and where the explanation for the treatment is unsatisfactory or lacks cogency or credibility.

Statutory Rights: Collective Rights

The fourth cornerstone right is the collective rights of trade unions and employee representatives to play an active role in redundancy proposals where twenty or more redundancies are planned.

Again, these laws have been around since 1971, are reasonably well known and well established. Collective rights still present a major risk to HR Practitioners.

The reason why they present a risk is that the award for a failure to comply with the requirements is a punitive award against the employer. An employer may be made to pay up to ninety days pay per employee in favour of a group of employees whom have not received proper consultation through their representatives, either elected or trade union.

Collective rights of consultation are mandatory where twenty or more employees are being dismissed at one establishment in a ninety-day period.

Typically, an employer will have to consult collectively where a site is closing.

We will cover collective rights to consultation in a later chapter.

So, we can see that during a redundancy exercise an employer has to be alive to a whole host of risks relating to employees' rights.

In essence these rights are all about treating employees fairly during the exercise. If the mindset is fairness and treating employees how the practitioner would like to be treated then the risks should mitigate themselves.

CHAPTER TWO

REDUNDANCY PAYMENTS

Most people go to work to earn an income. If that income is no longer going to be present because the employee's job is redundant then the law has developed to provide compensation for that loss of job.

Losing a job through redundancy is seen as a no-fault job loss. The law provides a financial cushion to help the employee through that period. That financial cushion is known as the redundancy payment.

Individual employees are not responsible for societal technological progress that may render the employees' job obsolete, nor are they responsible for economic contractions which may render their jobs as not financially viable.

There are two key sources of a redundancy payment:

1. Statutory Redundancy Payments. Parliament has legislated for a minimum redundancy payment where an employee loses their job through redundancy.

2. Contractual Redundancy Payments. Some employers, mainly larger employers or employers with recognised trade unions, have redundancy payment schemes that exceed the statutory minimum schemes. Contractual schemes provide a bigger financial cushion to soften the blow of loss of employment income. Some contractual redundancy schemes are so attractive that some employees, particularly those nearing the end of their employment careers, are only too willing to be made redundant as

the redundancy lump sum provides a degree of financial security which would otherwise be unavailable.

Statutory Redundancy payments first featured in the 1965 Redundancy Payments Act. The provisions of that Act have survived, largely unaltered, and been transposed into successor legislation – The Employment Protection and Consolidation Act of 1978, which was superseded by the Employment Rights Act of 1996. This area of law has not seen many seismic changes which means this book won't go out of date quickly.

In order to qualify for a redundancy payment an employee has to get over four hurdles:

1. The employee has to show that he or she has been dismissed.

2. The employee has to show that he or she has two years service at the relevant date.

3. The employee has to show that the dismissal is solely or mainly attributable to redundancy.

4. The employee has to show that he or she has not unreasonably refused an offer of alternative employment.

1. Dismissal

This term has, with some exceptions, exactly the same meaning as unfair dismissal law. For those interested you can find the exact definition for redundancy purposes at section 136 of the Employment Rights Act 1996 and for unfair dismissal purposes at section 95 of the Employment Rights Act 1996.

Dismissal means:

1. Dismissal either with or without notice of termination. Where dismissal is without notice there would usually be a payment in lieu of notice. Volunteering for redundancy can amount to a dismissal. If an employee has been given notice of termination and commits an act of gross misconduct during the notice period then an employer can dismiss summarily and the dismissal will be by reason of gross misconduct and will extinguish any right to a redundancy payment.

2. Dismissal where the employer has breached the contract fundamentally entitling the employee to leave with or without notice. A constructive dismissal by reason of redundancy is a relatively rare circumstance but could arise where an employer unilaterally tries to alter an employee's role fundamentally, for example by taking away a manager's reports, and the employee resigns in response to the breach. Arguably that unilateral change amounts to a dismissal and the reason for the change is in effect redundancy. In reality the statutory redundancy payment is calculated in exactly the same way as a basic award for unfair dismissal.

3. Dismissal on expiry of a fixed term contract without such contract being renewed on the same terms.

Section 136 (5) of the Employment Rights Act 1996 also provides that some events will automatically amount to a dismissal for the purposes of a statutory redundancy payment. These include the death of an employer where an employee is employed by a sole trader. Where a school amalgamates into another school such an amalgamation may amount to a dismissal.

A dismissal will also vanish if an employee accepts a suitable offer of alternative employment at the conclusion of a trial period.

We will look at alternative employment in greater detail but accepting suitable alternative employment has the effect of making the dismissal vanish. That makes sense because a dismissal is a loss of employment. A re-instatement on the same terms or a re-engagement on different terms means continued employment.

A dismissal will also vanish if an employee is re-instated on internal appeal against redundancy selection. If there is no dismissal there is no entitlement to a statutory redundancy payment. The redundancy payment vanishes with the dismissal.

There will be no dismissal where an employee is warned of pending redundancies but decides to leave by resigning.

Provided that the employee is not under an employer notice of termination that employee will be taken to have jumped and not been pushed by the employer.

This is a problem for employees as many employers, consistent with both good practice and legal obligations, will inform employees of a department closure or a site closure many months before the closure takes place.

Some employees will seek to gain a head start in the job marketplace by looking for alternative employment. If they are successful in obtaining another job and give notice to their employer they will not establish any right to a redundancy payment as they will not have been dismissed.

In larger scale redundancy exercises with long lead times employers may wish to make clear to employees that leaving too early may disqualify them from a statutory redundancy payment.

2. Service

An employee needs at least two years service to qualify for a redundancy payment. The practitioner needs to establish the employee's start date. That should be relatively straight forward as the start date should be in the employee's section one statement of terms and conditions.

The service needs to be computed to the relevant date. The relevant date is:

1. Where notice has been served the expiry date of that notice. So, if one month's notice was given on 1 May that notice would expire on 31 May. 31 May would be the relevant date and the effective date of termination.

2. Where no notice has been served but the employee has been dismissed immediately, or where less than statutory notice has been served and the employee has been paid in lieu of notice, then the relevant date is the date statutory notice would have expired had it been given. Statutory notice is one week's notice per year of service capped at 12 weeks. If an employee is entitled to longer contractual notice, that is immaterial, the relevant date is calculated to the date statutory notice would have expired had it been given.

3. That employee would have been entitled to 2 weeks statutory notice. His service is therefore calculated up to 14 May.

The relevant date only becomes relevant where there is an employment anniversary or, in some cases, the employee's birthday falls between the effective date of termination and the relevant date.

Service needs to be continuous. Where an employee works for associated employers, for example, different companies within a group of companies, service is aggregated from the start date of employment.

Special rules apply to calculating service in local government, some schools and the NHS, where service can be aggregated between different employers.

Some service is discounted. In summary discounted service is:

1. Any day that the employee has been on strike. Strike days come off the total service.

2. Any service for which the employee has already received a redundancy payment.

3. Any week where there has been no contract of employment breaks continuity of service. There are saving provisions that save broken continuity. Those saving provisions are notoriously fact sensitive so if there is a query about broken service which may be continuous take legal advice.

3. By reason of redundancy

Redundancy has a particular definition for redundancy payments and unfair dismissal purposes – the primary definition.

For collective consultation purposes there is a broader definition that captures more circumstances than the primary definition – the wider definition.

Starting with the primary definition, the wording of this definition has remained undisturbed since 1965.

It is worth setting out section 139 of the Employment Rights Act 1996 in full:

> *(1) For the purposes of this Act an employee who is dismissed shall be taken to be dismissed by reason of redundancy if the dismissal is wholly or mainly attributable to—*

(a) the fact that his employer has ceased or intends to cease—

(i) to carry on the business for the purposes of which the employee was employed by him, or

(ii) to carry on that business in the place where the employee was so employed, or

(b) the fact that the requirements of that business—

(i) for employees to carry out work of a particular kind, or

(ii) for employees to carry out work of a particular kind in the place where the employee was employed by the employer,

have ceased or diminished or are expected to cease or diminish.

So, in summary, in order to qualify for a statutory redundancy payment an employee has to be dismissed wholly or mainly by reason of redundancy. Redundancy means:

1. The employer has ceased or intends to cease business (the business is shutting).

2. The employer has ceased or intends to cease business at the employee's place of work (the workplace is shutting).

3. The employer has no requirement or a reduced requirement for a particular job (the job is going).

The business closing entitles the employee to a redundancy payment, if the employee is subsequently dismissed. A business may close for a number of reasons:

1. An insolvency event: An insolvency event is defined as bankruptcy in the case of a sole trader employer, or administration and liquidation in the case of a limited company

employer. If the employer is insolvent, appointed licensed insolvency practitioners and has no funds to make a redundancy payment, the employee can claim a redundancy payment from the Redundancy Payments Service (RPS). The claim can be made online and will usually take between 4 to 8 weeks to process.

2. Business decision to close: then unless there is no buyer the employee will be entitled to a redundancy payment.

The second type of redundancy situation is the workplace closing.

A workplace closing can be for a number of reasons. These include:

1. An employer has a large factory and needs to downsize to a smaller factory in the same city. On the face of it this amounts to a redundancy situation as the workplace is closing. However, an employee may not be entitled to a redundancy payment if:

    a. The employer offers the employee his job in the new location on the same financial terms. Whether this amounts to a suitable offer will depend on the employee's own situation. If the new location is closer to the employee's home address then the offer is likely to be suitable. If the new location is further away from the employee's home address then the offer may either be unsuitable or it may be unreasonable for the employee to refuse the offer. Much will depend on the employee's individual circumstances. The more the employer does to assist employees to get to work at the new location the harder it will be for the employee to argue he is entitled to a redundancy payment. For example, if the employer either offers transport to the new location or a travel allowance then it will be difficult for the employee to argue that they are entitled to a redundancy payment.

    b. The employee has a mobility clause in the employee's contract. If the employee has specifically agreed in his contract that he will work either at location A or any other location within 5 miles of A, then if the new location is within 5 miles of A the employer could rely on that mobility clause to move the employee to the new place of work. If the mobility clause in the contract is less specific and says that the employer can require the employee to work at any of the employer's locations in the UK, it is harder for the employer to rely on that clause to require the employee to move to a different site. A mobility clause cannot easily defeat an entitlement to a redundancy payment (see Bass Leisure v Thomas.)

So, the employer closing for business or closing a site is relatively straightforward. The employees affected will be entitled to a redundancy payment unless there is a TUPE situation in the case of the employer closing or the employer has another site where employees can be transferred in the case of a workplace closing.

The third scenario is the one that causes the most debate and has generated the most caselaw.

In order to meet the definition there has to be (or there is expected to be) fewer employees carrying out work of a particular kind.

The first step is to identify what the employee whose role you are considering making redundant actually does. The case law was unclear for a number of years but is now settled. In order to determine the work of a particular kind an employee does the test is a factual one, what does the employee do, rather than a contractual one, what is he or she contracted to do or could be contracted to do. Contracts are drafted to allow for an employee to do anything that could be reasonably expected of him or her.

The general trend in employment law is to recognise that employers draft the contracts and the contracts may not reflect the actualitē.

Therefore, factual tests are used to look at what the employee actually does in the workplace rather than what the employee could be required to do under the contract.

That makes sense. An employment relationship is dynamic. An employee may join, have a contract, and then over the years of service be given additional duties and responsibilities, or even a different job title and the contract may not be updated or -reissued to reflect those changes.

Let's look at some scenarios of "work of a particular kind" to flesh this out.

An employer that re-furbishes office equipment may employ two typewriter repairers. As very few offices now have typewriters to repair and the demand for refurbished typewriters no longer exists at a sufficiently high enough rate, then an employer might declare those two posts redundant. The employer has no requirement for typewriter repairers and that job no longer is required within the business. Straightforward redundancy, no issues.

If, however the two typewriter repairers spend 25% of their time mending typewriters and 75% of their time re-furbishing computer keyboards but there is only enough work for one employee then again it is straightforward to reduce the numbers by one.

If, however, the employer employs 10 Office Peripheral Repair Operatives to repair and refurbish a whole range of office equipment including typewriters then work of a particular kind is wider. If the overall repair work is decreasing the employer will need fewer operatives and can reduce the numbers and meet the definition for redundancy.

A more common but difficult scenario is where the employee is re-organising its work processes and decides that they need different sorts of employees with different or slightly different job descriptions and responsibilities.

So, for example a manufacturing employer may have a factory employing 10 shift supervisors. The employer may re-organise their processes and decide that rather than 10 shift supervisors they need 10 team leaders.

The employer could declare the 10 shift supervisor roles as potentially redundant and place the employees doing those jobs at risk of redundancy.

The employer would or could invite all 10 at risk employees to apply for the new team leader role.

If 8 out of the 10 at-risk shift supervisors were successful at interview and appointed then the two unsuccessful at-risk employees would be entitled to a redundancy payment as on the face of it the requirement for employee to do work of a particular kind, shift supervisor, has ceased or diminished.

If the employee then claimed unfair dismissal based on the new job being no different to the old job and the selection process being unfair for the new roles, then the employer would argue that there was a genuine redundancy situation and a fair selection process, and in the alternative that if redundancy is not established as a reason for dismissal then in the alternative the reason for dismissal is some other substantial reason, in this case re-organisation.

If the Employment Tribunal found that there was not a redundancy but a re-organisation because the particular work of a team leader is very similar to a shift supervisor, then the practical impact on the employer is that the employer would not be able to offset the redundancy payment paid to the employees against any basic award for unfair dismissal.

In effect by wrongly labelling the dismissal as redundancy rather than re-organisation, the employer deprives himself of the right to offset any redundancy payment against the basic award [see Boorman v Allmakes Limited [1995] IRLR 553].

If an employer wants to change the hours of an employee and the change amounts to a reduction then the employee can reuse the request and say that such a change amounts to a redundancy situation. The case of Mr Ron Packman t/a Packman Lucas Associates and Ms P Fauchon established that a reduction in hours amounts to a redundancy situation entitling the employee to a redundancy payment.

Timing

The wording of the statute is predicated on the facts known to the employer at the point notice is given.

It is not that uncommon for an employer to make redundancies because of a shortfall in orders and then shortly after the expiry of the notice period of those employees made redundant the employer receives orders and then has a requirement for employees.

The fact that unexpected orders arrived after the date that notice of termination expired does not make a difference to the fairness or otherwise of the redundancy dismissal.

Therefore, an employer might make a post redundant based on reasons x, y and z. After two months the employer might realise they have made a mistake and then advertise for a person to fill the position.

Provided there is a supervening set of facts which changes the employer's thinking, unknown to the employer at the point of dismissal but occurring after dismissal, then an employer is free to recruit into a role that they have made redundant.

There is no safe period after which an employer can recruit. The key issue is: has something happened after a redundancy dismissal to change the employer's mind about the redundancy. If something has happened then an employer can recruit for the role.

Unreasonable refusal of a suitable alternative employment

As discussed above many employers will offer employees whose posts are redundant alternative employment.

An employee if he or she decides they would like to accept an offer of alternative employment would usually be offered a trial period of 4 weeks.

Trial periods can be longer than 4 weeks by agreement if longer there is usually provision for the employee to default back to a redundancy payment if the trial is unsuccessful. 4 weeks is the statutory minimum.

So, if a warehouse operative is being made redundant from a factory as the employer needed fewer warehouse operatives the employer may offer a job within the factory as a factory operative.

Provided the financial terms and other terms were either similar to or identical with the factory operative role then this offer is likely to be a suitable offer, an employee would need to have a reasonable reason to turn it down.

An unreasonable rejection of a suitable offer may disqualify an employee from a redundancy payment.

Many employers would still nonetheless make the redundancy payment, notwithstanding the fact that an employee has turned down an offer of continued employment, albeit in a different job.

Similarly where an employer closes a site but re-opens a bigger (or smaller) site in the same town or city and offers every employee a job in the new location, then subject to all financial terms and hours being the same, an employee could only reasonably turn down such an offer if the new location meant a longer commute to and from work each day.

The key points on suitable alternative employment are:

1. Is the new job objectively suitable? That involves looking at the terms and conditions, in particular the financial terms. If the salary or hourly rate is lower the offer is likely to be unsuitable.

2. How reasonable is it for the employee to refuse the offer? Reasonableness is a subjective test and will depend on the employee's own circumstances and aspirations.

Most employers will pay a statutory redundancy payment even though the employee may have refused an offer of alternative employment, suitable or otherwise.

Enhanced Redundancy Payment

Larger employers may have a contractual redundancy payment scheme. Contractual redundancy payment schemes are most often found where the employer has a recognition agreement with a Trade Union and in the public sector.

The most common types of enhancement are:

1. To remove the cap of weekly pay and make the redundancy payment based on actual pay – for example if the employee's actual gross weekly pay is £750.00, it is that amount that is used rather than the current cap of £643.00.

2. To increase the number of weeks pay for each year of service. Some employers in the banking sector pay out a month's pay for each year of service but then put a cap on the number of months in total for example a month for every year of service capped at 24 months.

Enhanced redundancy terms become contractual in a number of ways:

1. There is a collective agreement on enhanced redundancy pay and that collective agreement applies to those job roles in a bargaining unit. That collective agreement becomes incorporated into the individual's contract of employment. Some professions or job types had agreed redundancy terms for example printers or journalists. The National Union of Journalists had agreed with many employers in publishing that journalists, if they were made redundant, would receive a month's pay for every year of service.

2. The enhanced terms are set out in a handbook, redundancy policy or redundancy procedure and the handbook or policy and procedure is incorporated into the contract of employment. See Keeley v Fosroc International Ltd 2006 IRLR 96.

3. By the implied term of custom and practice, in order for an enhanced redundancy payment to become implied into the contract it has to meet the test set out in the case of Quinn and Ors v Calder Industrial Materials Ltd 1996 IRLR 126. In that case a policy to pay an enhanced redundancy payment had not become contractual. In order to become contractual a policy had to be:

    (a) Followed without exception over many years.

    (b) Communicated to employees.

    (c) Intended to be contractual.

It is quite difficult for an employee to establish an implied term of custom and practice of an enhanced redundancy payment as it is in the employer's gift to break the custom. A few examples where an employer has used a different calculation methodology will break the custom.

Lay off and Short Time Working

Employers who have a sporadic order book or work volumes that fluctuate can give themselves the right in the contract of employment to put employees on lay off or short time.

The employer having the right to lay employees off or put them on short time working is prevalent in some industry sectors, for example the automotive industry. It enables the employer to cut its cost base to meet a shortfall in work and income, whilst retaining a skilled workforce.

Lay off is defined as no work in a particular week, short time is defined as working sufficiently less than a full contracted week for pay to drop to less than half a week's pay.

However, once an employee has been on 4 consecutive weeks of lay off or short time working or 6 non-consecutive weeks of lay off or short time in a 13 week period, the employee has the right to request from the employer a statutory redundancy payment.

The rules on an employee requesting a redundancy payment are highly prescriptive and technical involving the employee giving written notice within 7 days of the end of the qualifying period. The qualifying period are 4 weeks for consecutive lay off or short time or 13 weeks in the case of non-consecutive lay off or short time working.

The employer has the right to reject a written request for a statutory redundancy payment. The employer's right to reject is similarly prescriptive. The employer must use a written counter-notice. The reason for the rejection has to be that the employer will be able to resume full time working within 6 weeks of the end of the qualifying period.

Additionally, the employee has the right to a guarantee payment for the first 5 days of lay off or short time in a 3-month period. A guarantee payment is uprated each year and in 2023 is £35 per day or your daily rate whichever is lower.

We have seen in this chapter that an employee has an entitlement to a statutory redundancy payment or an enhanced redundancy payment if certain conditions are met. In the next chapter we will look at implementing a redundancy plan to reduce the numbers of employees employed.

CHAPTER THREE

DECLARING REDUNDANCIES BELOW TWENTY EMPLOYEES

We have established how an employee becomes entitled to a statutory redundancy payment. In this chapter we will look at how an employer can effect fewer than twenty redundancies and not breach any redundant employee's right not to be unfairly dismissed.

An employee has the right to claim unfair dismissal if they have 2 years' service at the effective date of termination [EDT]. The EDT is the date the employee leaves employment. The EDT can be and often is a different date to the relevant date.

In most cases the EDT will be one of the following:

1. The last day of employment where the employee leaves and is given a payment in lieu of notice.

2. The last day of the notice period where the employee is given notice of termination and either works their notice period or goes on garden leave for the duration of their notice period.

The only exception to the above rules on establishing the EDT is where an employee is paid in lieu of notice within a week of their two-year service qualification period.

Where an employee achieves two-years service on say 1 May, then any dismissal, with a payment in lieu of notice that takes place in the week before the 1 May will mean that the employee qualifies. This is because section 97 of the Employment Rights Act 1996 is engaged which allows for the EDT to in effect be extended by a week where dismissal without notice but with a payment in lieu takes place within a week of the two-year qualifying period.

Two years is the qualifying period for ordinary unfair dismissal but for automatic unfair dismissal there is no service qualification.

Automatic unfair dismissal includes selection for redundancy based on one of the following:

1. Whistleblowing.
2. Health and safety activities.
3. Shop workers who refuse Sunday work.
4. Activities relating to enforcing working time rights.
5. Participation in statutory training and education.
6. Activities of trustees of occupational pension schemes.
7. Employee representative activities.
8. Asserting a statutory right.
9. National Minimum Wage activities.
10. Tax Credit activities.
11. Flexible working activities.
12. Blacklists.
13. Pension enrolment.
14. Trade Union activities.

The law intervenes to give special protection from dismissal for those who partake of certain activities that are allowed by law (see above list). Those employees should not be dismissed or selected for redundancy for taking part in those activities.

An employer should review whether any employee falls within one of the above categories. Making a complaint about health and safety does not prevent the employee from being selected for redundancy, it does prevent the employee from having the fact of the complaint about health and safety tainting their selection for redundancy.

Furthermore, an employee (as well as workers) have the right not to be discriminated against during a redundancy exercise. The right not to be discriminated against does not have a service qualification.

Therefore, because redundancy involves a dismissal and the loss of employment, sensible employers will try to treat all employees who are at risk of redundancy in the same way or a very similar way, regardless of length of service.

Treating the employees the same way enables the employer to learn at the earliest opportunity whether any at risk employee considers themselves automatically unfairly dismissed or discriminated against.

An employer taking a short cut by not allowing any individual consultation rights to employees with under two years' service deny themselves the right to nip any discriminatory dismissal or automatically unfair dismissal in the bud.

One of the key cases for redundancy unfair dismissal is Williams and others v Compare Maxam Limited [1982] ICR 156.

That case laid down some general principles. These are:

1. The employer will seek to give as much warning as possible of impending redundancies so as to enable the union and employees who may be affected to take early steps to inform themselves of the relevant facts, consider possible alternative solutions and, if necessary, find alternative employment in the undertaking or elsewhere.

2. The employer will consult the union as to the best means by which the desired management result can be achieved fairly and with as little hardship to the employees as possible. In particular, the employer will seek to agree with the union the criteria to be applied in selecting the employees to be made redundant. When a selection has been made, the employer will consider with the union whether the selection has been made in accordance with those criteria.

3. Whether or not an agreement as to the criteria to be adopted has been agreed with the union, the employer will seek to establish criteria for selection which so far as possible do not depend solely upon the opinion of the person making the selection but can be objectively checked against such things as attendance record, efficiency at the job, experience, or length of service.

4. The employer will seek to ensure that the selection is made fairly in accordance with these criteria and will consider any representations the union may make as to such selection.

5. The employer will seek to see whether instead of dismissing an employee he could offer him alternative employment.

As workplaces have become less unionised over the years, in the absence of a trade union an employer may wish to consult at stages 1 and 2 of Compare Maxam above either the works council or forum if they have jurisdiction on consultation over proposed redundancies or alternatively the at-risk pools of employees directly.

One of the most cited cases in unfair dismissal claims is Polkey v AE Dayton Services Limited 1988 ICR 142. That case established that procedural fairness is a key part of whether an employer is within or without the range of reasonable responses. A failure to follow the correct procedures will make redundancy dismissals unfair unless following those procedures would have been "utterly useless." There are not many scenarios where it would be utterly useless not to follow any procedure.

The law will not enquire too closely into the reasons for declaring redundancies, unless there is an allegation that the redundancies are a sham or cover for discriminatory conduct.

This is as it should be. In a free-country employers should be allowed to make business plans and not have the reason for those business plans judicially scrutinised, unless it is absolutely necessary.

Employers are free to make business plans and then implement those plans, even if those plans turn out to be disastrous. It's not as if the UK does not have a track record of disastrous business plans.

Coupled with that a business does not need to be in a financially critical situation in order to declare redundancies. Many highly profitable, cash rich businesses can and do declare redundancies. In short, an employer is free to make and implement plans.

What the law does look at is the process of how the business plan to reduce headcount by declaring redundancies is implemented. Redundancy, just like any other reason for dismissal, is all about the procedure and process an employer follows. No process or no procedure will almost certainly render a dismissal unfair.

There are a number of key mindsets that employers should adopt during the redundancy process. These are:

1. Management does not have the monopoly of wisdom or judgment. Employees doing the job at the coal face may be in a better position to spot flaws and weaknesses in a plan to reduce jobs than an accountant sat at a desk, poring over a spreadsheet under an angle poise lamp deciding that x thousand pounds and y number of posts needs to come off the monthly costs.

2. Plan, consult and then decide, in that order. For many employers the process is: plan, decide, and then consult. That is the wrong way round. Many unfair dismissal judgments contain the phrase: "Consultation is the cornerstone of good industrial relations practice."

3. Consultation where there are fewer than twenty redundancies is a qualitative process rather than a quantative one. Not unlike other workplace activities, consultation is not about how long it lasts but about how much respect, listening and consideration there is. Employees like to feel that their points are being engaged with, their voice is being heard and their input taken seriously. Employees who do not consider their input has either been sought or considered are more likely to seek advice on their situation.

The classic statement on consultation is one given by in the case of R v British Coal Corporation ex parte Price and Others [1994] IRLR 72:

> *Fair consultation will involve consultation while consultations are at a formative stage; adequate information on which to respond; adequate time in which to respond and conscientious consideration by an authority of the response to consultation. Applying the test in R v Gwent ex p Bryant: 'It is axiomatic that the process of consultation is not one in which the consultor is obliged to adopt any or all of the views expressed by the person or body whom he is consulting. 'and' Another way of putting the point more shortly is that fair consultation involves giving the body consulted a fair and proper opportunity to*

> *understand fully the matters about which it is being consulted, and to express its views on those subjects, with the consultor thereafter considering those views properly and genuinely.'*

So, whilst that case involved collective consultation, there is if not a requirement certainly an expectation to consult for unfair dismissal purposes where fewer than twenty employees are being made redundant.

Consultation follows a less prescriptive form where fewer than twenty employees are being made redundant. In order to ensure that the dismissal is fair, there should be consultation.

The key to consultation is:

1. Plan.

2. Consult.

3. Decide.

In that order.

An employer has some latitude in how consultation is carried out where there are fewer than twenty redundancies planned.

There is no definitive correct process that has to be followed. Many lawyers could suggest different ways. However in my view the best way of handling a sub-twenty redundancy is:

1. Management formulate a plan comprising of:

    a. Numbers of employees to be made redundant.

    b. Pools from which those employees form a part.

    c. Selection Criteria to be used.

   d. Timetable for achieving the reduction.

2. Management consult the at risk pools regarding the plan.

3. Following consultation management make the selections.

4. Management consult individually those selected.

5. Those selected have their contracts terminated if their selections are confirmed on conclusion of individual consultation.

We will look at various scenarios on how to conduct a small scale, sub-twenty, redundancy exercise.

In all of the various scenarios below we are working on the basis that the employer does not have a redundancy policy and procedure, in which case that should be followed. We are also working on the basis that there is no collective agreement with a recognised trade union on how redundancies should be effected.

If we look at a scenario where an employer employs 5 sales ledger clerks and 5 purchase ledger clerks but because of the introduction of new scanning technology that can scan and input purchase invoices as well as sales invoices, the requirement for clerks diminishes by 5.

There are a number of ways this reduction can be effected. There is no one definitive correct process. I will give two possible ways of effecting the reduction.

The first way is to select using selection criteria with the bottom 5 being selected for redundancy. The second way is to select all 10 for redundancy and give all of those selected an opportunity to apply for one of the new posts. I will not deal with the mechanics of selection in this chapter, that comes in chapter 5.

I will look at the consultation process. Consultation is absolutely key.

In my view the best way is to follow the following timeline:

1. Day One: Convene a meeting of all 10 finance clerks. The line manager should explain the following at that meeting

    a. That new technology is being introduced which will mean that only 5 clerks will be required.

    b. That in the first instance volunteers are being sought.

    c. Any application for voluntary redundancy must be put in writing to the line manager by day 3.

    d. The employer reserves the right to refuse any application for voluntary redundancy on the grounds of operational efficacy.

    e. That volunteers if accepted will receive a payment in lieu of notice, a statutory redundancy payment, and a volunteer's premium of £x.

    f. That if insufficient volunteers are received the employer intends to apply the following selection criteria on day 4. The proposed selection criteria should be published.

    g. That all employees in the affected group are invited to comment on the selection criteria.

    h. That if compulsory selections are necessary those provisionally selected for redundancy will have an individual consultation meeting on day 5.

    i. At the individual consultation meeting provisionally selected employees will be given a copy of their own scores, together with an anonymised league table giving a relative position in the pool. Any vacancies will also be shared at this meeting.

j. There will be a second individual consultation meeting on day 7 at which the employee will be given an opportunity to challenge their scores and inform the employer of whether they are interested in any alternative employment that is available.

k. On day 8 there will be a third individual consultation meeting at which the redundancy will be confirmed or otherwise.

l. On day 10 those employees whose redundancies have been confirmed will leave the employer with a payment in lieu of notice and a statutory redundancy payment.

2. Day Three: consider volunteers for redundancy. If sufficient suitable volunteers, this brings the redundancy exercise to a close. If insufficient volunteers the employer applies the redundancy selection criteria and makes provisional selections. Obviously the selection criteria should only be applied after feedback from the at risk group on the draft selection criteria.

3. Day Five: First individual consultation meeting with those provisionally selected for redundancy. Share with them their scores and an anonymised league table. Share with them the details of any alternative employment that is available. Explain that the second individual consultation meeting on day 7 will give the employee an opportunity to either agree with or challenge any scores. The second meeting will also give an opportunity for the employee to express an interest in any alternative employment.

4. Day Seven: Second individual consultation meeting. The employee's opportunity to give feedback on the scores awarded as well as express an interest in any alternative employment.

5. Day Eight: Third individual consultation meeting. The employer feeds back on the points raised by the employee at the second individual consultation meeting and either confirms or reviews the provisional selection or progresses any interest in alternative employment. The outcome is confirmed in writing, together with details of any appeal procedure.

6. Day Ten: Those provisionally selected leave the business with a payment in lieu of notice as well as any statutory redundancy payment.

7. Days 12 to 20: any appeals against redundancy selection are heard.

Whilst an employer could probably get away with a shortened version of this timeline, this sort of procedure minimises the risks of any successful legal challenge and maximises the prospect that all employees involved will feel fairly treated.

Situational psychology is important. By giving an employee the right to volunteer the employer cedes some control to the employee. By allowing the employee to feel in control of their fate minimises an adversarial response. Employees can present to family and friends that they have been offered a generous package for voluntary redundancy and they have taken the decision to apply for voluntary redundancy. Saying that you have volunteered for redundancy rather than being compulsorily selected is a lot easier for the employee's self-esteem and well-being.

Secondly, by announcing both the proposed selection criteria and the volunteer's premium for a successful application for voluntary redundancy an employer can nudge an employee into self-selecting for redundancy.

By announcing the proposed selection criteria and scoring mechanism the employee should be able to calculate or predict their chances of being selected or retained. If the employee feels that there is a pretty good chance based on the proposed selection criteria that they will be selected for redundancy it would be irrational not to volunteer. An employee would be better off volunteering than being compulsorily selected.

Legally, an employee who volunteers for redundancy will face an up hill struggle to win an unfair dismissal claim, so accepting applications for voluntary redundancy reduces legal risks for the employer as well as giving the above benefits for the employee.

The second way the reduction in accounts personnel could be achieved is to put all 10 employees at risk of redundancy and invite all 10 to apply for the 5 new roles. The timeline would be similar to making selections using selection criteria.

1. Day 1: Convene a meeting of all 10 finance clerks. The line manager should explain the following at that meeting:

    a. That new technology is being introduced which will mean that only 5 clerks will be required. Those 5 clerks must have the ability to do both sales ledger and purchase ledger work. The job description for the new roles is given to each at risk employee.

    b. That all 10 employees are at risk of redundancy.

    c. That all 10 employees will have the opportunity to apply for one of the 5 finance clerk roles.

    d. All 10 employees must notify the line manager by day 3 either whether they wish to apply for the new clerk role or whether they wish to leave as redundant. Such notification should be done by completing a preference form – the choice is between applying for the new role or leaving as redundant.

e. Any employee who wishes to leave as redundant will receive an enhanced redundancy payment consisting of a payment in lieu of notice, a statutory redundancy payment, and a leaver's premium of £x.

f. That if more employees apply for the 5 vacant roles then selection for those roles will be carried out by competency based interviews.

g. Interviews for those who have applied for the 5 vacant roles will be carried out on days 4 and 5, with candidates notified of their result on day 6.

h. Those who are unsuccessful at interview will have three consultation meetings on days 6 and 8 and 10.

i. At the first individual consultation meeting unsuccessful employees will be given feedback on the competency interviews. Any vacancies will also be shared at this meeting.

j. There will be a second individual consultation meeting on day 8 at which the employee will be given an opportunity to challenge the feedback and inform the employer of whether they are interested in any alternative employment that is available.

k. On day 10 there will be a third individual consultation meeting at which the redundancy will be confirmed or otherwise.

l. On day 10 those employees whose redundancies have been confirmed will leave the employer with a payment in lieu of notice and a statutory redundancy payment.

2. Day 3: consider applications for the 5 vacant posts. If there are 5 or fewer applicants, this brings the redundancy exercise to a close.

Those who have applied for the 5 posts can be slotted into role, those who have opted to leave can leave with a payment in lieu of notice, a statutory redundancy payment and a leaver's premium.

3. Day 3: If there are more than 5 applicants for the vacant roles then the applicants can be interviewed by way of a competency based interview on days 4 and 5.

4. Days 4 and 5: Competency based interviews are carried out with the line manager and one other manager. Successful and unsuccessful candidates are notified of the results.

5. Days 6: First individual consultation meeting. The employee is given feedback on the interview as well as notified of any alternative employment.

6. Day 8: Second individual consultation meeting. The employee feeds back on the interview feedback as well as notifying the employer of any interest in any other alternative employment.

7. Day 10: The employer feeds back on the points raised by the employee at the second individual consultation meeting and either confirms or reviews the result of interview or progresses any interest in alternative employment. The outcome is confirmed in writing, together with details of any appeal procedure.

8. Day 10: Those unsuccessful at interview leave the business with a payment in lieu of notice as well as any statutory redundancy payment.

9. Days 12 to 20: any appeals against redundancy are heard.

This sort of competitive interview process is what many employers use. There is one considerable drawback for the employer though. The employer cedes all control to the employee. In particular the employees control who remains within the business. It is not unusual for the best employees to opt not to apply for one of the vacancies. Those employees will then be lost to the business. Furthermore, those who do apply for the vacancies may not be employees who would have got through a compulsory selection process via selection criteria as per scenario one. Sometimes less capable or confident employees stick with what they know rather than throwing themselves into the employment market.

Where there is a recognised trade union then the day one meeting would normally be held with a trade union official present.

Similarly, if there is a works council or employee forum that within its constitution is consulted over redundancies, then the contents of the day one meeting would normally be shared with the employee forum before it takes place, with the forum given an opportunity to put any points over.

Obviously, there is an issue of confidentiality as the forum members will have knowledge of the redundancies in advance of those affected. That is unavoidable. An employer would normally require all forum members to keep the contents of the discussion confidential until the employer had had the opportunity to consult with the at-risk group.

The third scenario is where there is a one-off discrete redundancy effecting a reduction of one employee but with two employees at risk. That finance function may have a Finance Director and a Finance Manager who reports to the Finance Director. The employer may wish to reduce its costs and change the organisation by having a Financial Controller and a Credit Controller both reporting to the Manging Director.

In that scenario the process would be along the following timeline:

1. Day One: Meet with both the Finance Director and Finance Manager either individually or as a group. Explain the following:

a. That the Employer is proposing to have a re-organisation.

b. That the re-organisation proposes to remove the role of Finance Director and Finance Manager.

c. That the re-organisation proposes to replace those roles with the roles of Financial Controller and Credit Controller.

d. That the reasons for the re-organisation are: to reduce cost and flatten the structure.

e. The job descriptions of both new posts. Hand out these out, together with an indication of the remuneration package.

f. Both employees have an opportunity to come back to the employer with written comments and representations on the proposed re-organisation, together with any suggested alternatives by Day Three.

g. The Employer will consider any comments made and come back to the employees on Day Five.

h. Subject to a decision being made to go ahead with the proposal both employees must indicate whether or not they wish to apply for and be considered for either or both roles by Day Seven.

i. The process for recruitment into the new roles will be by way of a competency based interview.

j. If neither employee wishes to be considered for either role, then the roles will be advertised externally and when appointments are made into the new roles both employees will be allowed to leave with a statutory redundancy payment and a payment in lieu of notice on an agreed date.

k. If one or both employees wish to be considered for either or both roles, arrange an interview. Internal applicants will be considered and interviewed before the roles are thrown open to external candidates.

2. Day Three: Conscientiously consider any representations made by the employees.

3. Day Five: Go back to either or both employees with written responses to any representations made with a rationale as to why the representations are accepted or rejected in full or in part.

4. Day Seven: Consider any applications from either at risk employee for either role.

5. Thereafter: arrange interviews, conduct interviews, and make appointments into role. Agree termination dates and handover arrangements with any at risk employee who is leaving.

Consultation is the key to a fair process.

Consultation is usually in two stages: The first stage with the affected group, the second stage with those individually selected for redundancy from the affected group.

We have seen above how a group consultation is conducted. A group consultation explains the rationale for the proposal to make redundancies, the proposed methodology for implementing the redundancies, together with the proposed timeline.

A group consultation allows the affected employees time to consider the proposals and come back to the employer with any suggestions, views or alternatives.

By allowing the affected employees to have input into both the proposal to make redundancies and the proposed methodology for effecting the selections, the at risk employees are buying into the whole process. The affected employees will have some ownership of the process as they will have had an opportunity to influence the proposal before it becomes a decision.

In my view the consultation in advance of the selections is a crucial step not only to ensure any subsequent dismissal is fair but as part owners of the methodology to make selections, it is difficult for the employee subsequently to argue that the methodology was unfair. The selected employees will have been part of the decision-making process in constructing the method of selection.

Once the group stage of consultation is concluded and the employer has made a decision not only to make redundancies but also the method of making them, the employer must make the selections.

Once those selections have been made, the employer must consult individually an employee selected for redundancy. We will consider individual consultation in further depth in a later chapter, but the consultation covers two issues:

1. The selection:

    a. If it is a one-off post being removed the consultation on selection is limited to why that post is going and where the tasks associated with that post are being distributed to. However, as we have seen above in the example of the finance director and finance manager the rationale for the redundancies will already have been explained, with the employee already having had the opportunity to make any representations. The individual consultation meetings will be limited to a reiteration of that rationale together with looking at arrangements for terminating the employment.

    b. If an employee is being selected from a pool then the selection criteria scores, together with anonymised league table, are normally shared with the employee in order for the employee to understand why he has been selected and give the employee an opportunity to challenge the scores.

2. Alternative employment. An employer should normally cover what alternative employment is available, if any, either within the business or within any associated business. An employer should not assume that an employee will not be interested in alternative employment, even if that alternative employment is at another location and involves either a demotion or a pay cut. Employees should be given the opportunity to consider any post that is vacant. There will be some posts that will not be suitable, based on skills or experience.

Having conducted hundreds of Employment tribunal claims for employers, I learned that many claims are upheld because the employer has not consulted properly. Proper consultation also avoids the risk of unfair selections for redundancy as the employee will have had an opportunity to input into the proposed design of the selection process.

Whilst not all practitioners will agree with the following steps, in my view the following steps combine the legal with the ethical:

1. Prepare a plan and timeline for reducing headcount.

2. Consult the affected group about the plan and timeline.

3. Make the selections.

4. Consult those selected.

5. Terminate the contract of any employee whose selection is confirmed following individual consultation.

Collective consultation which we will look at in the next chapter follows broadly similar steps.

CHAPTER FOUR

DECLARING REDUNDANCIES OF TWENTY OR MORE EMPLOYEES – COLLECTIVE CONSULTATION

We have seen what the law of unfair dismissal says about the need to consult. We have seen that where fewer than twenty redundancies are proposed an employer should, in my view, consult the at-risk group with the proposed plan, before implementing the plan.

Where twenty or more redundancies are proposed the obligations are more prescriptive. The law recognises that employers making redundancies impacts the geographic area those employers are situated in and therefore makes bigger demands. In particular, the law requires an HR1 Form to be submitted to a government department. An HR1 Form enables government functions such as Job Centres to know in advance that a large number of people may be needing their services. Failure to submit an HR1 is a criminal offence.

In many towns and cities one large employer dominates. That employer sustains many households, those households spend their money in many local businesses.

An employer has responsibility for its employees. The employer provides an income that will help to provide for the employee's household, keep a roof over his or her head and put food on the table.

In the Victorian era some employers, in particular those businesses owned by Quakers such as Cadbury's, Unilever, and Reckitt and

Coleman, took their responsibilities as employers extremely seriously to the point that the employers even built houses for their workforce.

Such commitment from employers has been eroded in what is now an extremely competitive market economy where employers are producing goods or services and customers are deciding between competing products and services, partly on price.

The cost of employees' labour is a key component in pricing a good or service. There is a relentless drive to become more competitive and more efficient. That drive impacts on an employer's ability to provide security of employment. Redundancies are an inevitable part of the onward march of progress.

The European Union has recognised this. The EU has also recognised that the relative bargaining position between employees and employers is asymmetrical. The European Union has therefore tried to, if not level the playing field, make the playing field have less of a slope. It has tried to make the playing field less asymmetrical.

The European Union has through a series of directives given employees rights in the workplace. These rights trump any contrary term in the contract. Member states have to implement directives into domestic law within 2 years of being passed.

Whilst the UK has had a long tradition of trade unionism in the workplace, collective consultation rights on making more than twenty redundancies were initially limited to those employers who had recognised trade unions.

In the UK there has sometimes been a gap between an EU Directive and a UK law implementing a directive.

Such a gap was present in the UK's transposition of the collective redundancies directive.

The primary gaps were a failure to allow for collective consultation to a workforce who did not have Trade Unions recognised for collective bargaining purposes, the level of compensation for those who have not been collectively consulted correctly and crucially the meaning of redundancy.

The current law on Collective Consultation is contained in the Trade Union Labour Relations (Consolidation) Act 1992 or TULR (C) A. The provisions are at section 188 onwards.

Crucially the definition of redundancy is wider than under UK domestic law.

As we have seen in UK domestic law the right to a redundancy payment is engaged where a dismissal is attributable to a redundancy situation – a workplace closing, an employer closing or the need for an employee to do work of particular kind reducing.

The requirement to collectively consult is engaged where an employer is proposing to dismiss twenty or more employees as redundant at one establishment within a ninety-day period.

Taking the definition of redundant first, that is defined at section 195 (1) which states:

> "*References to dismissal as redundant are references to dismissal for a reason not related to the individual concerned or for a number of reasons all of which are not so related.*"

You do not need to be particularly eagle eyed to notice that that definition is far wider. It includes the definition of redundancy for redundancy payment purposes but it also includes broader re-organisation dismissals which may not meet the definition of redundancy for redundancy payment purposes. The upshot is that you could be an employee who has collective consultation for redundancy but may not be eligible for a redundancy payment if you are dismissed by reason of the wider definition of redundancy.

The best way of explaining the difference and illustrating it is by way of a real case example. In GMB v Man Truck and Bus Limited 1999 EAT 971/99 the employer wanted to introduce new terms and conditions for part of its workforce. The workforce did not agree to the change and the employer then gave all employees affected notice of termination of their contracts of employment with an offer to re-engage on different terms on expiry of the notice period.

None of the employees were entitled to a redundancy payment as none of the dismissals were attributable to a redundancy situation as defined for redundancy payment purposes.

However, the affected employees were entitled to have collective consultation carried out by their employer with the recognised trade union, the GMB. The reason for this is that the employees' dismissals met the wider definition of redundancy at section 195 (1).

Similarly, if an employer tries to impose new terms and conditions on a workforce, such an imposition can amount to a dismissal (see Alcan Extrusions Limited v Yates) and such dismissals would be by reason of redundancy as the dismissals relate to a workforce or part of workforce wide changes to terms.

If employees do not agree to changes to terms and conditions, the employer can terminate their contracts and offer to re-engage on new terms.

The requirement to consult collectively is engaged where the employer is proposing to dismiss twenty or more employees as redundant within a ninety-day period.

Redundant means situations where a redundancy payment would be due, as well as wider re-organisations which may not result in redundancy payments being due.

So, the requirement to consult is engaged where there is a:

1. Proposal to dismiss as redundant either twenty or more employees or one hundred or more employees at one establishment. Dismiss means with or without notice, constructive dismissal, and expiry of a fixed term. Propose has been the subject of much caselaw but it means where the employer has a definitive proposal to make redundancies. It also means the obligation to consult is engaged **before** any decisions to make redundancies are taken.

2. Redundant means more than just a reduction in employees, it can be a situation where the number of employees is static but their terms and conditions need to change.

3. Within a ninety-day period means proposals to dismiss are aggregated over a ninety day period to see whether the obligation to consult is there. Employment Tribunals are alive to the possibility that some employers wish to avoid consulting so chop redundancies up into batches of fewer than twenty and roll those batches out over time.

When does an employer need to consult?

Where there are twenty or more redundancy dismissals at one establishment but fewer than one hundred proposed at least thirty days before the first proposed redundancy dismissal takes effect.

Where there are one hundred or more redundancy dismissals proposed at least 45 days before the first proposed redundancy dismissal takes effect.

This does not necessarily mean that consultation has to last thirty days and forty-five days respectively, the employer and the employees' representatives could agree that consultation can end before thirty days and forty five days are up.

An employer would not be wise to give any affected employee notice of termination whilst consultation is ongoing with employees' representatives.

What does one establishment mean?

The answer to this depends on the facts. Some employers have one site and the answer is straightforward, a site and an establishment are the same thing. Other employers have employees spread across several sites or spread around the UK in regional offices.

Is a regional office an establishment or is the UK business the establishment? The answer depends on a number of factors including whether there is an autonomous decision-making ability at the regional office, who has the power to declare redundancies, whether there is an identifiable economic unit.

Of course, if there are more than twenty redundancies at one site the obligation is engaged. But if the number of redundancies at any one site are fewer than twenty but when aggregated with other sites more than twenty then you will need to take legal advice to understand whether consultation requirements are engaged or not. Every case is very fact sensitive and different.

The safest route is if in doubt consult collectively. Consulting collectively may add two to four weeks onto the process but does mitigate the substantial financial risk of not consulting collectively.

Whom does the employer need to consult?

The employer needs to consult the affected employees' recognised trade union or their elected representatives. If the employees are not in a workplace where trade unions are recognised or involved then the default position is to consult with their elected representatives.

Elected representatives are either an employee forum or works council, provided that forum or council has jurisdiction to be consulted over collective redundancies. An employer needs to check the council's or forum's written constitution to ensure that consultation over redundancies is within their remit.

If there is no written constitution then the employer should arrange for the election of representatives. Election of reps and voting has some pedantic and technical rules and legal advice should be sought. Each department or function affected by the proposal to make redundancies should elect at least one representative if not two per department.

Elections may not be necessary where only two candidates put themselves forward to stand per department.

Every workforce has natural dividing lines or boundaries which are understood and recognised. Office workers and factory workers in a manufacturing environment. Managers and office workers in a call centre. If the redundancies are spread throughout the workforce, care should be taken to ensure that each area affected has at least one elected representative.

What is the purpose of consultation?

The purpose is three-fold:

1. To avoid, minimise or reduce the numbers to be dismissed.
2. To mitigate the consequences of each dismissal.

3. To reach agreement as far as possible on the subject matter of what is being proposed.

How should consultation be carried out?

The law is clear. Consultation should be carried out with a view to reaching agreement. Obviously, an employer can only reach agreement if they have only formalised plans and proposals.

An employer cannot reach agreement on a decision already taken. On site closures where the lease on premises may be up for renewal, an employer needs to consult before it takes a decision on whether to renew the lease. Consulting after a decision has been taken negates the purpose of consultation. Those consulted will have no ability to put points forward as to why the site should not close.

One practical point which sometimes catches employers out is board meeting minutes. Board meeting minutes need to describe any decision taken at board level. However, redundancy declarations are normally board level decisions.

Therefore, any decision to declare redundancies is a decision to declare redundancies only, not to effect redundancies. The board should decide that they need to declare redundancies and such a declaration needs to go to either the trade union or the employee representatives for consultation. The board decision should be to propose redundancies but to consult with the appropriate representatives over numbers, timeframes and methodology of selection.

If political moves to obtain employee representation at board level are enacted, then board meetings will in future have more employee involvement in decisions that affect the whole workforce.

Special care needs to be taken where an employer is also a listed public company as market sensitive information needs to be disclosed to the market in accordance with that market's rules.

The mantra remains the same though: propose, consult, decide – in that order.

What information needs to be given?

The law is prescriptive as to what information needs to be given to the trade union or employee representatives. There are some specific and technical rules on service of the information and legal advice should be sought.

Firstly, the information should be given in writing.

Secondly whilst an employer can give the information out in chunks, best practice is to give the information out in one document.

The information that needs to be given is as follows:

1. The numbers of employees to be made redundant together with their description as well as the numbers and types of agency workers and where those agency workers are working. The best way of getting that information over to the representatives is by way of a table. The table should show where the redundancies fall. The table may look something like this where the requirement is to reduce the workforce by a third:

Department	Post Numbers	Proposed reduction
Sales:	20	5
Finance:	10	3
Production:	110	30
Warehouse:	20	7
HR:	3	1
Technical:	10	3
Quality/HSE	5	1

If an employer wanted to give more information, then they could break the jobs down within each department so that the table for the sales department might look something like this:

Department	Post Numbers	Proposed reduction
Sales	Sales Director	0
Reducing by 5 from 2015.	1	
	Account Managers	2
	14	
	Sales Support	3
	5	

Obviously, the more detail an employer can give the better informed the employees are. The better informed the employees are the more in control of their own individual situation they will feel. Obviously if one method of effecting the reduction is to seek volunteers first, the more detail that can be given the better.

2. Reasons for the redundancies: An employer has to give the reasons for the redundancies. The reasons may be mixed, for example to increase profitability as well as to reduce cost to allow capital expenditure on productivity enhancing machinery and equipment.

3. Proposed method of carrying out the redundancies: this means the proposed selection criteria. The proposed selection criteria may be:

   a. Volunteers first from at risk job groups.

   b. Then selection criteria which could be:

      i. Skills.

      ii. Attendance.

      iii. Length of service.

      iv. Disciplinary record.

      v. Last appraisal rating.

4. Proposed timetable: That usually means the date of the first proposed redundancy dismissals. From the employees' perspective they will want to know when will employees selected for either voluntary or compulsory redundancy be allowed to leave. Will they be dismissed with notice? Or without notice but with a payment in lieu of notice? If with notice, will employees be expected to work their notice or will they be put on garden leave?

Employees should give as much information as possible so that employees can make an informed decision as to whether they will volunteer for redundancy or take their chances on not being compulsorily selected.

5. Proposed method of calculating redundancy payments. This needs to be fully detailed for example will the employer be paying statutory redundancy payments only? Will the employer be paying enhanced redundancy payments? If so, how will the enhancements be calculated? Will the employer be paying the same level of redundancy payments to volunteers as well as those compulsorily selected? Will volunteers receive a premium to incentivise volunteers to come forward?

The collective consultation usually takes place with a series of meetings over a number of weeks. The meetings should be minuted or at least noted and where possible those minutes or notes should be agreed at the start of each meeting. Best practice is to ensure that every employee in an at-risk pool should also receive minutes of each meeting so that they can feedback to their representative any comments, queries or suggestions.

Common tactics from the employer's perspective is to over declare redundancies at the start of consultation only to concede during consultation and reduce the proposed numbers of redundancy dismissals. Some employers also start consultation with the worst possible financial proposal, only to give way during consultation.

For example, some employers may start collective consultation with a proposal only to pay statutory redundancy payment but then concede during collective consultation to pay redundancy pay based on actual pay not capped pay. Alternatively, some employers may start the collective consultation process with the proposal to make employees work their notice only to accept during collective consultation to pay employees in lieu of notice.

An employer, consistent with the case law definition of consultation, should give conscientious consideration to all the points made by the elected representatives. The employer should come back at the next meeting giving rationales for why those points are accepted or rejected. Sometimes points may be accepted in part.

The range of consultation covers all of the information that the employer is required to give in writing. Representatives may have representations to make about any or all of the rationale for redundancies, the pooling, the selection criteria, the proposed method of carrying out the dismissals or the proposed payments.

The employer needs to be open minded enough to accept that their proposals may have flaws and those flaws may be pointed out by the representatives. A certain amount of humility is required. An employer should stop digging if they are in a hole rather than use the spade to bludgeon the representatives into accepting proposals that don't cut the mustard.

There comes a point during collective consultation where every point that could be agreed has been agreed and every point that has not been agreed there is an agreement to agree to disagree. Elected representatives are not readily going to agree the numbers of redundancies or the need for redundancies. They will always suggest alternatives to employees losing their livelihoods.

There is nothing, in principle, preventing the elected representatives or trade union officials from agreeing that collective consultation is at an end and that the employer can move on to applying the selection criteria and then individually consulting those provisionally selected.

Such an agreement should be in writing and preferably signed by all the parties.

The collective consultation process should be about agreeing, as far as possible, the framework and methodology for effecting the redundancies. The consultation should be about the big picture as it applies to the group rather than looking at individuals within the group.

Separate requirement to notify

Where twenty or more redundancy dismissals are planned at one establishment there is a separate requirement to inform the Department of Business, Innovation and Skills on form HR1 of the numbers, pools, proposed selection criteria and timetable.

The employer should also give the appropriate representatives a copy of form HR1.

Getting it wrong

Either an elected representative or a recognised trade union can make an application for a protective award to Employment Tribunal. There are limited circumstances where an individual employee can make a claim for a failure to consult collectively.

Such an application does not have to go through ACAS early conciliation.

Such applications are usually made if:

1. The employer has not collectively consulted at all. Some employers either don't consult at all taking a risk that they are breaching the law. A small number of employers are unaware of the obligation. Some employers if they are in financial dire straits or have had a receiver or administrator appointed will take immediate action to reduce headcount, as they do not have the financial resources to consult over a timeframe.

2. The employer has not collectively consulted properly. These sorts of claims can be because the employer has already decided to

close a site and then collectively consults about the decision. Or because collective consultation has not taken place when proposals are at their formative stage. Or because all of the required information has not been given to the elected representatives.

Awards for a successful claim for collective consultation are known as protective awards. The award is punitive in nature. The award is made for a number of days pay and it is made in favour of a class of employees who should have had collective consultation. It is then up to each of those employees to make an application to Employment Tribunal to claim the protective award.

The award can be up to ninety days pay. However, if the default by the employer is minor or technical, the award can be as low as one day's pay. Crucially the award is made for a class of employees so can amount to a considerable sum, even if the award is not the full ninety days pay.

Are there any defences?

Yes – an employer can plead the statutory defence of there being special circumstances that excuses them from the requirement to consult collectively. Such special circumstances are few and far between. Examples of exceptional circumstances are usually financial for example if an organisation is on the point of insolvency and the pay for the consultation period would push them into insolvency, that would be an exceptional circumstance which would excuse a collective consultation process.

What happens after collective consultation is concluded?

The employer is free to apply the selection criteria and commence individual consultation with those who are provisionally selected for redundancy. The elected representatives will not normally be involved with the individual consultation process. However, some employers will check with the elected representatives whether they agree that the selection process has been applied in accordance with the agreed methodology.

So collective consultation where there are twenty or more redundancies planned is similar to group consultation where there are fewer than twenty redundancies planned. The process is similar in format in that:

1. Formulate a written plan about how to achieve the reduction. The written plan should contain all of the required information at section 188.

2. Consult the appropriate representatives of the affected employees, either the recognised trade union, or the elected representatives or both where one part of the affected workforce has a trade union recognised and another part does not.

3. Start the consultation process by giving the appropriate representatives the written plan which covers all of the section 188 bases.

4. At the same time submit form HR1 to the department of BIS. Give a copy to the appropriate representatives.

5. Meet the appropriate representatives with an open mind.

6. Conscientiously consider any points made. Agree on any agreed points in writing. Agree on where you disagree in writing. Conclude collective consultation.

It is at this point an organisation moves on to the crunch part of the process, making the selections.

CHAPTER FIVE

POOLS, SELECTION CRITERIA AND SELECTION

An organisation is like an organism, it needs to adapt to survive. The market economy is Darwinism in action, only the fittest employers prosper, the weak get eaten or die.

The public sector economy is dependant on the political will of government. Priorities and willingness to commit expenditure varies from government to government and from political party to political party.

A redundancy exercise is well named, it is just like exercise in that the aim should be to remove the fat and leave the muscle, to make the employer stronger and leaner afterwards.

Just like exercise there is a need for focus. An organisation needs to identify which parts of their corporate body they need to work on.

There are three discrete but interlinked activities – determining the pool, establishing the selection criteria, and applying the selection criteria.

The Pool

Firstly, the pool – the law is settled. Provided an employer considers the issue of a pool and consults either with the group affected or with the elected representatives on the pool, then an Employment Tribunal will not interfere. The leading cases say that if an employer does not consider the issue of the pool then the dismissal is likely to be unfair.

In Mogane v Bradford Teaching Hospitals NHS Foundation Trust and another [2022] EAT 139 a nurse whose fixed term contract was up for renewal at the same time a redundancy situation arose, was pooled as one and made redundant solely on the basis that her fixed term contract was due to be renewed soonest.

It was held the dismissal for redundancy was unfair and another nurse on a fixed term contract should have been within the redundancy pool. Before any genuine and meaningful consultation took place or meetings as to the selection criteria to be applied, it was decided that the nurse whose fixed term contract was up for renewal should be the nurse who is dismissed. The tribunal found there was insufficient consultation on the pool. If you have a pool of one you need to give more consideration to the employee during consultation if they make points about why they should be pooled with other employees.

Where there is a custom or arrangement regarding pooling then an employer should stick with that custom unless there is good reason to depart from it.

Provided an employer can show that they have applied their minds to the issue of pool, consulted on proposed pooling then it will be quite difficult for an employment tribunal to substitute their own judgement on pooling with that of the employer.

Let's flesh this out with some examples.

A factory might have 5 electrical engineers and 5 mechanical engineers to service, maintain and repair machinery in a factory. The machines have become more reliable and the need for service, maintenance and repair has reduced.

The electrical engineers have not been trained and do not do mechanical engineering and vice versa.

On closer investigation of the data the employer finds that electrical faults and repairs are far more common than mechanical faults.

Therefore, the employer proposes to reduce the mechanical engineers by 2 and the electrical engineers by 1. The pools look like this:

Job Title	**Present**	**Future**	**Surplus**
Mechanical Engineers	5	3	2
Electrical Engineers	5	4	1

If the mechanical engineers and the electrical engineers had interchangeable skills – with mechanical engineers able to do some electrical engineering and vice versa, then an employer could still pool as above, or alternatively could pool like this:

Job Title	**Present**	**Future**	**Surplus**
Engineers – Mechanical/Electrical	10	7	3

It would be up to the employer to decide the pool, after consultation, and an Employment Tribunal cannot readily interfere with the decision and substitute their own view.

Assume an employer operated a three-shift system: day shift being from 6am to 2.00pm, afternoon shift being from 2.00pm to 10pm and night shift being from 10.00pm to 6am. There are 4 engineers on each shift – 2 electrical and 2 mechanical, except for night shift where there was two engineers one mechanical and one electrical. The employer does have the right in the contract to move employees between shifts with agreement but in practice rarely exercises that right.

An employer could reasonably exclude the night shift workers from the pool and make the selection from the day and afternoon shift workers engineers only.

The pooling would look like this adopting either methodology:

Job Title	**Present**	**Future**	**Surplus**
Mechanical Engineers – day shift/ afternoon	4	2	2
Electrical Engineers – day shift/ afternoon	4	3	1

Or if interchangeable the pool would look like this:

Job Title	**Present**	**Future**	**Surplus**
Engineers – Mechanical/Electrical – day shift/afternoon	8	5	3

If the employer needed at least one mechanical and one electrical engineer on shift at night, then excluding night shift engineers from the pool is entirely reasonable.

Including them in the pool could leave the employer operationally exposed if one or both night shift engineers are selected for redundancy and no other engineer agrees to work night shift.

Let's look at another example, service engineers. An employer manufactures telephone switchboard equipment which is installed at customers' premises throughout the UK.

The employer has home based service engineers spread throughout the UK like this:

Region	Number of Service Engineers
North Scotland	1
Central Scotland	2
Southern Scotland and Borders	1
North West England	4
North East England	4
Yorkshire and Humberside	4
Lincolnshire	1
East Midlands	3
West Midlands	4
East Anglia and Essex	3
North Wales	1

South Wales	2
Bristol and West	3
Devon and Cornwall	1
South Coast West and South West	2
South Coast and South East	3
London	5
Southern Home Counties	3
Northern Home Counties	4

The Company has reviewed utilisation of service engineers and found that every region that has one service engineer, that service engineer is under-utilised in terms of number of jobs carried out each year.

How does the employer deal with this?

Well there are a number of ways:

Firstly, it could decide to treat each region with one engineer as a discrete pool and make each engineer in that pool redundant. The pool would look like this:

Region	**Present Number of Service Engineers**	**Future Number of Service Engineers**	**Surplus**
North Scotland	1	0	1
Central Scotland	2	2	0
Southern Scotland and	1	0	1

Borders			
North West England	4	4	0
North East England	4	4	0
Yorkshire and Humberside	4	4	0
Lincolnshire	1	0	1
East Midlands	3	3	0
West Midlands	4	4	0
East Anglia and Essex	3	3	0
North Wales	1	0	1
South Wales	2	2	0
Bristol and West	3	3	0
Devon and Cornwall	1	0	1
South Coast West and South West	2	2	0
South Coast and South East	3	3	0
London	5	5	0
Southern Home Counties	3	3	0
Northern Home Counties	4	4	0

The service engineers would instinctively understand the pooling as they are assigned to a geographic patch. However, a service engineer in a redundant region is likely to say who will cover my region? The answer to that is the nearest geographically placed engineer. So, jobs in Southern Scotland and the Borders will be covered by any available service engineer either from Central Scotland or North West England or North East England.

That being the case, there is an alternative way to pool which is to put service engineers from adjoining geographic areas in the pool. The pool would look like this:

Region	Present Number of Service Engineers	Future Number of Service Engineers	Surplus
North Scotland	1	0	1
Central Scotland	2	2	0
Southern Scotland and Borders	1	0	1
North West England	4	4	0
North East England	4	4	0
Yorkshire and Humberside	4	4	0
Lincolnshire	1	0	1
East Midlands	3	3	0
West Midlands	4	4	0
East Anglia and Essex	3	3	0
North Wales	1	0	1
South Wales	2	2	0
Bristol and West	3	3	0

Devon and Cornwall	1	0	1
South Coast West and South West	2	2	0
South Coast and South East	3	3	0
London	5	5	0
Southern Home Counties	3	3	0
Northern Home Counties	4	4	0

In this pooling exercise the employer is pooling by those regions affected. Those regions affected are those regions which would cover the work after a particular region loses a service engineer.

The third way of creating a pool is to pool all engineers nationally. There would be 47 engineers in the pool and a requirement to reduce by 5. The 5 lowest scoring engineers would be provisionally selected for redundancy. In order to make this pool work operationally an employer would have to ensure that the selection criteria chosen to select the engineers for provisional redundancy are fit for purpose.

The selection criteria must leave the right number of service engineers in the right geographic locations. One way of doing that would be to choose selection criteria that would achieve that. For example, scoring service engineers by the number of customers within 60 miles of their home location. The service engineers with the fewest number of customers within 60 miles of their home location would be provisionally selected for redundancy.

An employer with a geographically diverse workforce has a number of ways of achieving a reduction in terms of which pool to adopt. The key is to ensure that the employer has considered the issue carefully, consulted with the at-risk group on the issue of the proposed pool and made a decision on which pool to use following consultation.

Another pooling conundrum is where the same type of employee does the same or similar work for a particular department.

Does an employer pool by department? Or does an employer pool across departments?

Let's flesh this out into an example. A board of directors has 7 directors. Each director, with the exception of the Managing Director, has responsibility for a department. The departments are: sales, operations, quality and technical, marketing, HR and finance. The Managing Director has each Director report into her.

The business needs to reduce costs. It has been decided that the number of secretaries should be reduced and that in the future the Managing Director will have her own secretary, and thereafter the remaining six directors will have three secretaries between them.

Does the employer ringfence the Managing Director's secretary from consideration from redundancy? The answer is probably yes as the Managing Director would argue that it is important for her to have continuity of support and that she has built up a rapport with her secretary that would be difficult to replicate.

There are several different ways of achieving the reduction.

You could have pooling like this:

Post	**Present**	**Future**	**Surplus**
Secretary to Managing Director	1	1	0
Secretary to Sales Director	1	0	1
Secretary to Finance Director	1	0	1

Secretary to Operations Director	1	0	1
Secretary to Quality and Technical Director	1	0	1
Secretary to HR Director	1	0	1
Secretary to Marketing Director	1	0	1

The obvious problem with this pooling is that all of the secretaries in surplus posts may decide to leave the employer with a redundancy package, leaving 3 Directors' Secretaries posts that would need to be recruited into externally. That may not suit the employer.

However, another way of pooling would be to pool across departments and pool like this:

Post	**Present**	**Future**	**Surplus**
Secretary to Managing Director	1	1	0
Departmental Director secretaries	6	3	3

The employer using the above pooling mechanism would ensure that they would be left with 4 secretaries after the selection exercise-the Managing Director's secretary, with 3 other secretaries remaining after the selection exercise.

In my experience there are more issues over selection criteria and their application than there are about pools. If the employer has consulted the group about the proposed pool prior to applying the selection criteria it is difficult for an Employment Tribunal to interfere with the pool that the employer uses. Employment Tribunals are not allowed to substitute their own pool but simply decide whether or not the pool used was reasonable. A range of reasonable responses test is used. A decision of an employer will be outside the range if no employer would have acted or decided in that way. It will be within the range if some employers would have decided that way and other employers would not have.

At employment tribunal a pool will be outside the range of reasonable responses if no employer would have adopted the pool used. That is a low bar for the employer to get over.

Selection Criteria

This falls into two discrete issues: the selection criteria and the application of the selection criteria.

An employer does have free rein, within limits, to choose its own selection criteria. As set out in the previous chapters on consultation an employer should consult the affected group about the proposed selection criteria. Not only does consulting the affected group give the employer advance warning about any deficiencies in the proposed selection criteria and an opportunity to amend those criteria before use, it also gives the employer buy in from the affected group that the selection criteria that are to be used are effectively agreed. Achieving this buy in makes it harder for an employee to say that the selection criteria themselves are unfair. Furthermore, it allows those affected some say in their future by allowing them input into the best way of determining who should stay and who should be made redundant. Employees are quite capable of being objective in this situation and in dividing their own situation from what's best for the organisation.

As we have seen above on pooling with the service engineers, an employer could pool those service engineers nationally and then apply completely objective selection criteria to achieve the required reduction. The example given above was to use the selection criteria of number of customers within a 60-mile radius of the employee's home address. To add further sophistication an employer could also add in a weighting to the criteria as to the financial value of that customer, as well as whether that customer also had planned and paid for maintenance visits as part of its service arrangements, together with number of call outs and visits per year that customer had.

In that those customers with a high financial value would achieve a greater score than those with a lower financial value. Similarly, those customers that required more paying visits could be weighted higher than low maintenance customers.

A number of general observations at this point. If an employer were to use such selection criteria, it is absolutely critical that the data that is being used to support the scoring is accurate.

Therefore, before applying the criteria during the group consultation stage it would be sensible for the employer to check with the affected group that it has the correct home address of each service engineer. This is basic but basic detail is easily overlooked.

Secondly an employer needs to be sure that the data about its customers is accurate and up to date.

Thirdly an employer needs to measure over an agreed reference period. The usual reference period would be the 12 months immediately preceding the redundancy. Therefore, if redundancies were declared on 1 March 2025, the reference period for scoring the number of customers within a 60-mile radius of a service engineer's home address would be 1 March 2024 to 28 February 2025.

A need to reduce service engineers is a pretty specific redundancy reduction.

If the pooling was not done nationally but by regions affected, then an employer could still use the selection criteria of number of customers but may wish to ensure that the best service engineers were retained which may not necessarily be those who live in a geographically convenient and densely populated with customer's location.

There are a number of types of selection criteria that can be used. Scoring can either be positive or negative.

It is essential that the employer defines what each criterion means so that there is no ambiguity as to definition.

The sorts of criterion that are commonly used include:

1. Technical Skills – does the employee have particular skills for example on product lines. So, with the service engineer example above you could break down this criterion into the product lines. Employees who have skills on product lines that are legacy products i.e. installed at a customer's premises but have been superseded by more up to date technology may score lower than employees having a skill on more up to date product. An employee with skills and experience across the product range may score higher than an employee with skills on one part of the product range.

2. Technical Skills – if the employee works in an office environment as a secretary as per the above example, does the employee have the full range of skills on the Microsoft Office Suite product? Or are their skills limited to Word and Outlook. A secretary who was fully skilled and experienced in Word, Outlook, Excel and PowerPoint may score higher than an employee who is just skilled on Word. How many words per minute can the secretary type? Can they take shorthand?

3. Quality of work – is the employee's output always at a high standard? Or are there concerns about quality? Does the employee's work ever need re-doing? Are there many mistakes? Are there any or many customer complaints?

4. Quantity of work – does the employee get a lot, a little, or an average amount done in a working day?

5. Qualifications – does the employee have formal educational qualifications or technical qualifications on a particular product, or both.

6. Performance – how has the employee performed during the reference period? Does any formal performance documentation exist, such as appraisal documentation?

7. Attendance – days – has the employee been off sick, how many days has the employee been off sick?

8. Attendance – instances – How many instances of sickness absence has there been over the reference period?

9. Disciplinary – has the employee had any disciplinary offences and sanctions within the 12-month reference period? If so, what was the sanction?

10. Timekeeping – does the employee keep good time or are they ever late? Are there records to capture timekeeping, such as clocking in and out records or door entry records?

11. Flexibility – is the employee flexible? Does the employee take on additional duties or work additional hours to assist the organisation?

12. Communication skills – how good is the employee at communicating verbally or in writing?

13. Length of service – how long has the employee been employed?

These are examples of selection criteria that employers commonly use to make selections for redundancy. Much will depend on the individual business and what the needs of the business are. In essence what the selection criteria are doing is ensuring that the employees most able to meet the future needs and demands of the organisation are retained. The organisation is trying to retain employees who will assist the organisation to grow and achieve its goals in the future. Employees who have helped an organisation meet its goals in the past may not be the same employees who will be able to meet the organisation's future goals.

The selection criteria need to be able to retain model employees. In order to do that the organisation needs to know what the attributes are of a model employee.

Over the years I have seen organisations use attitude as part of their selection criteria. I have also seen appearance being used. That criterion measured how neat and tidy the employee was. That attribute was considered very important in a customer centric role.

An employer has considerable scope for determining the selection criteria to be used. Provided the selection criteria have been consulted on with the at risk group, it is hard for an employment tribunal to say such selection criteria are unreasonable. The employer needs to show a fair process, not a process that an employment tribunal would have used if faced with the same circumstances.

Applying the criteria

An employer must be able to show that the selection criteria have been objectively applied. An employer can have subjective criterion, such as attitude, but needs to be able to show that all selection criteria have been objectively applied and a consistent approach adopted.

Therefore, any HR Practitioner who is devising selection criteria needs to draft them in such a way as to eliminate or at least minimise the possibility of bias and subjectivity creeping in.

I have tended to favour hard scoring systems which forces the scorer to think about why an employee is being given a non- norm score.

Let's take a look at what I mean by that.

Some selection criteria for the secretary pool are detailed below. That's the pool where we are reducing the number of Director secretaries by three from seven to four. We are pooling all of the Director's secretaries as one pool, with the exception of the Managing Director's secretary who we have excluded from consideration.

Remember if these proposed selection criteria are given to the secretary pool as part of group consultation the scoring mechanism is reasonably transparent and it may well be that sufficient secretaries do the maths and instead of waiting to be compulsorily selected volunteer for selection. A voluntary selection is better for the employee as they feel more in control of their own situation and feel like that they have decided their own fate, rather than have their own fate decided for them. A voluntary selection is also better for the organisation as the reduction is achieved by voluntary means reducing the scope for conflict and dispute.

The proposed selection criteria could be something like this, although some employers might add other selection criteria depending on the needs of their business. Let's assume that the selection criteria proposed below leaves the organisation with the quickest, most accurate and most reliable secretaries. Those attributes are the ones most required by the organisation.

	Score		
Criterion	**1**	**5**	**10**
Length of service	Less than 2-years service as at 31 March 2025	More than 2-years service but less than 8-years service as at 31 March 2025	More than 8-years service as at 31 March 2025
Disciplinary record	A written warning that is live at any point in the reference period	An oral warning given in the reference period	No disciplinary issues in the reference period
Attendance: days	More than 5 days recorded sickness absence in the reference period	Between 1 to 5 days recorded sickness absence in the reference period	No recorded sickness absence in the reference period
Attendance: instances	More than two instances of sickness absence in the reference period	Two or fewer recorded instances of sickness absence in the reference period	No recorded instances of sickness absence in the reference period
Technical Skills: Microsoft Office Suite	Has used one MS Office application in the reference period	Has used two or three MS Office applications in the reference period	Has used the four main MS Office applications: Word, Excel, PowerPoint, and Outlook Office in the reference period

Examples and justification			
Technical Skills: Typing Speed	Can type audio but fewer than 80 words per minute	Can type audio between 80 and 119 words per minute	Can type audio at more than 120 words per minute
Examples and justification			
Technical Skills: Accuracy	Regularly makes typing mistakes	Makes some typing mistakes but not frequent	Never or very rarely makes typing mistakes
Examples and justification			
Flexibility:	Never works additional hours to get the job done	Sometimes works additional hours to get the job done	Regularly works additional hours to get the job done
Examples and justification			

So, if we look at the first four selection criteria those selection criteria should be based on data held by the organisation and should not be capable of challenge, except if there are some special circumstances that exist such as disability or maternity or if the data is inaccurate. Those four criteria should be scored by the HR department, if there is one, or by the person who has management responsibility for HR.

The last four criteria would be scored by each secretary's line manager who is a Director of a Department – HR, Finance, Operations and so on. There would be seven different scorers.

It has to be recognised that different line managers may have different standards. So in order to minimise the inherent subjectivity, each scorer would have to score using the same methodology.

The last four criteria are capable of more interpretation and judgement. It is usually better that a non-norm score – a 1 or a 10 – requires a written justification and examples on the score sheet. So, if a secretary scores a 1 or a 10 for flexibility the scorer, their line manager, would need to write some comments in the space provided in the box called examples and justification to justify their score. Writing concentrates the mind.

Feasibly typing speed and accuracy could be scored by asking all secretaries in the pool to type up the same audio tape of 5 minutes length and see how long it takes each secretary in the pool to complete. From that exercise one would have an objective score for both speed and accuracy. Alternatively, each line manager could score the secretary that works for them for speed and accuracy based on their own judgment and experience. That score may be capable of challenge but provided the examples are robust enough then any such challenge can be overcome.

The other benefit of the scoring system detailed above is firstly psychological – some secretaries can be selected who score a five or a ten for each criterion. The employee will feel that they are an excellent, reliable secretary who has narrowly missed out. A bit like not being good enough to play for Manchester City's first eleven but deserving a place on the bench.

The other primary benefit of using a one/five/ten scoring mechanism is that when the selected employees are met for individual consultation following their provisional selection the anonymised league table which each provisionally selected employee is given should show clear blue water between those selected for redundancy and those retained. By clear blue water those retained should have at least five marks if not more than those selected. Five marks are a lot of marks to make up as it means shifting one criterion's score from a five to a ten.

Those retained should have more scores of ten for more criteria and each score of ten puts five more marks distance between safety and selection.

Organisations are always sensible to have a tie breaker. Traditionally length of service is the tie breaker. If two employees were tied for selection, the employee with the longest length of service would be retained. Employers are, of course, free to choose whatever tie breaker they feel most meets their organisation's needs.

Common Issues with compulsory selection

Over the years a number of common issues have arisen with clients involving redundancy selection. These are:

1. The employer has not added up the scores correctly. This has happened and only been exposed during the Employment Tribunal hearing.

2. The definitions of the criteria are ambiguous. I have even seen the use of "etc" in the definition of a criterion. Different scorers will insert different things into what is covered by "etc." The definitions need to be tight so that each scorer is scoring the same thing.

3. The definitions for the criteria overlap. So, employees in the pool are being scored twice for the same thing.

4. The definitions of the scores are ambiguous. This is usually the case where the scores are as follows:

    a. Quality of work:

i. Score 1 mark if regular quality issues.

ii. Score 2 marks if frequent quality issues.

iii. Score 3 marks if occasional quality issues.

iv. Score 4 marks if infrequent quality issues.

v. Score 5 marks if no quality issues.

b. The problem with such a scoring mechanism is that the mark boundaries are too close together. A scorer can be easily tripped up under cross examination in the Employment Tribunal by being asked what's the difference between frequent and regular? Or what's the difference between infrequent and occasional? Most witnesses are insufficiently nimble to dance on the head of that particular semantic pin and will trip up answering such a question. That's why it is always best to have a hard scoring mechanism of 1, 5 and 10 which requires written justifications and examples for non-norm scores.

5. The woman on maternity leave. Special rules apply to making women on maternity leave redundant in connection with any alternative employment. Where a female employee is being scored for redundancy whilst off on maternity leave some allowance has to be made for the fact of maternity leave as the absence will disadvantage the employee. One way of dealing with this could be using the last full 12 months of employment prior to going off on maternity leave. The Protection from Redundancy (Pregnancy and Family Leave) Act 2023 that amends Part 5B Employment Rights Act 1996, may include provision for the protected period of pregnancy to begin after the end of pregnancy. If a female employee who is off on maternity leave is selected for redundancy, she would have rights under regulation 10 of The Maternity and Parental Leave Regulations 1999 [MAPLE].

6. The disabled person who takes sick leave. Most employers will disregard any disability related absence when scoring an employee's attendance. Failure to disregard disability related absence is very likely to be disability discrimination under section 15 of the Equality Act 2010. Alternatively, some employers will exclude from the pool anyone who is disabled. Positive discrimination in favour of disabled employees is permissible. An employer should take legal advice on how a disabled employee should be scored and what adjustments should be made. Employers are allowed to discriminate in favour of disabled employees and excluding disabled employees from the pool may be an option.

7. The short service employee may not have been there for the entire period of the reference period. How does an employer score such an employee given that the data is not there for the previous twelve months? There is no right answer. One way of dealing with the issue is to look at absence over the period of service and then pro-rata the data up for the full twelve months. Therefore, if an employee has six months service and has had three days of sick, then the number of days off sick for twelve months would be deemed to be six days.

8. The inconsistent performance documentation is a regular recurring feature of redundancy unfair dismissal claims. An employee has been scored using selection criteria and been selected for redundancy. That same employee has appraisal documentation within the reference period that shows good or excellent performance. The two issues are therefore inconsistent – the employee is not good enough to be retained under the selection criteria but is good enough to be given an above average performance rating under the performance appraisal system.

9. The biased manager crops up regularly – it is a difficult one to prove for the employee. However, employers should exercise care

and oversee diligently a manager who has been asked to score a pool of employees, one of whom has lodged a grievance against the manager recently. One case a few years ago an employee made out a claim for victimisation where she had lodged an equal pay grievance five years before her selection for redundancy. That equal pay grievance was a protected act. The employee's selection for redundancy was held to be an act of victimisation as her selection was tainted by the protected act, albeit that protected act was some way in the past.

10. There are particular groups of employees who are protected from unfair selection. They are those employees who have the right not to be automatically unfairly dismissed. An employer will need to review selections carefully to ensure an employee is not being selected for redundancy for carrying out protected activities, for example health and safety duties, or trade union duties.

It is important to note that the employment tribunal's role is to look at the system for selection rather than forensically re-examine each mark. An employment tribunal should only be looking at individual scores if there is a glaring inconsistency.

Selection by interview

In the case of the employer needing to reduce the number of departmental director secretaries by three, one way the employer could achieve that reduction is place all six secretaries at risk of redundancy and give all six secretaries an opportunity to apply for one of the three vacant roles. The vacant roles would be acting as secretary to two departmental directors rather than one.

We have already seen the obvious drawback from conducting the exercise in that the best secretaries may elect to leave the business with a redundancy package rather than apply for one of the vacancies.

Assuming that more than three secretaries applied for one of the vacancies, how should an employer conduct a selection interview. Following the case of Morgan v Welsh Rugby Union the Employment Appeal Tribunal held that the employer had a fair amount of discretion in how to hold selection interviews. An employment tribunal or court will not readily interfere into how such interviews are conducted.

An employer will, understandably, want to set up an interview selection exercise that is robust and ensures that the best candidates are selected for the vacant roles.

Such a selection exercise could consist of each interviewee being asked to type up an audio tape, followed by a competency based interview consisting of at least two interviewees.

An employer should ensure that accurate notes are kept of the selection process and that all appointments are made on merit. The employer should also feedback constructively to disappointed candidates as to why they had not been selected into role.

Summary

So, we have seen where an employer is faced with the need to reduce the number of employees the employer should:

1. Formulate a proposal to make the reduction.

2. Put the proposal in writing setting out key parts including numbers, pools, proposed selection criteria, call for volunteers and proposed time line for implementation.

3. Share the proposal either with the employees affected or their representatives.

4. Seek feedback and responses to the proposal.

5. Consider the responses and feedback replies.

6. Accept any volunteers.

7. Make selections.

Making selections should be a lot easier if the employer has consulted on the selection methodology with the affected group or their representatives. Consulting makes the design of the selection process a shared undertaking. Sharing the design with those affected enables buy in from those subsequently selected. They have helped to design the method of selecting for redundancy. They have been caught in a trap of their own making. The next stage is to consult individually with the employees who are provisionally selected for redundancy and that process is what we will look at in the next chapter.

CHAPTER SIX

INDIVIDUAL CONSULTATION

By now we are fairly well advanced in the process. We have included the affected employees or their representatives in every step along the way.

None of the information being imparted to those employees provisionally selected should be new.

As we have seen, lack of consultation may give rise to a claim especially when it involves an employee in a pool of one, as the employee can be unaware as to how the decision has been reached that they are the only person that makes up the redundancy pool.

If an employer has included all employees in consultation prior to any selection exercise being carried out and sought feedback from those in the pool on the proposals, including selection criteria, then individual consultation with any employee provisionally selected should be relatively straight forward.

The provisionally selected employee will be aware of the selection criteria. That issue will not need any further explanation. The focus of individual consultation is two-fold:

1. Firstly, to give the employee an opportunity to challenge or accept the scores awarded using the selection criteria. If the employee has been unsuccessful at a selection interview for a new role then the discussion is limited to feedback on how the employee performed during the selection process.

2. Secondly, to give the employee an opportunity to consider and apply for any alternative employment the employer has available.

Individual consultation is about a two-way exchange of information. Resist any temptation to use information as power.

In order to be able to discharge the individual consultation properly an employee should be given both a copy of their scores and a copy of an anonymised league table showing the employee where they are relative to other employees also in the pool. An anonymised league table in the secretary example above would look something like this for a Mrs Jones who has been provisionally selected:

Employee	**Scores for criteria 1 to 4**	**Scores for criteria 5 to 8**	**Overall score**	**Position**
xxx	25	20	45/60	1
yyy	20	20	40/60	2=
zzz	20	20	40/60	2=
aaa	20	20	40/60	4
Mrs Jones	16	12	28/60	5
bbb	10	15	25/60	6

Mrs Jones would also be given her score sheet which would have her individual scores for each criterion.

That score sheet may look something like the table below.

As you can see and Mrs Jones can see she has scored twenty eight out of a possible 60 and is 12 points away from safety. Even 12 points would put her equal with the employee who scored 40 points and she would be a subject to a length of service tie breaker.

Criterion	Score	1	5	10	Score
1	Length of service	Less than 2 years service as at 31 March 2025	More than 2 years service but less than 8 years service as at 31 March 2025	More than 8 years service as at 31 March 2025	1
2	Disci-plinary record	A written warning that is live at any point in the reference period	An oral warning given in the reference period	No disciplinary issues in the reference period	5
3	Atten-dance: days	More than 5 days recorded sickness absence in the reference period	Between 1 to 5 days recorded sickness absence in the reference period	No recorded sickness absence in the reference period	5
4	Atten-dance: instances	More than two instances of sickness absence in the reference period	Two or fewer recorded instances of sickness absence in the reference period	No recorded instances of sickness absence in the reference period	5
5	Technical Skills: Microsoft Office Suite	Has used one MS Office application in the reference period	Has used two or three MS Office applications in the reference period	Has used the four main MS Office applications: Word, Excel, PowerPoint, and Outlook Office in the reference period	1
	Examples and justifica-tion	Only uses Word			

6	Technical Skills: Typing Speed	Can type audio but fewer than 80 words per minute	Can type audio between 80 and 119 words per minute	Can type audio at more than 120 words per minute	5
	Examples and justifica-tion				
7	Technical Skills: Accuracy	Regularly makes typing mistakes	Makes some typing mistakes but not frequent	Never or very rarely makes typing mistakes	1
	Examples and justifica-tion	Have to correct spelling mistakes on letters			
8	Flexibil-ity:	Never works additional hours to get the job done	Sometimes works additional hours to get the job done	Regularly works additional hours to get the job done	5
	Examples and justifica-tion				

The purpose of individual consultation is twofold: firstly, the provisional selection for redundancy needs to be agreed if possible. Crucial to this is the free flow of information.

Employers all too often fall into the trap of thinking information is power and are not open and upfront in what they divulge. Some manager cannot resist the temptation of exercising power by not giving the selected employee information on their selection. That is a mistake.

Not only is a mistake it shows a lack of confidence in the process that the employer has followed. Being totally transparent about the process and open with the documentation not only shows confidence by management in the process followed but also gives the employee who has been selected confidence that the process is fair.

As Mrs Jones has already had sight of the proposed selection criteria prior to their application during the group consultation stage she is already privy to key information anyway. Furthermore, Mrs Jones will have been able to work out her own scores for most of the criteria as they are objective, data based scores.

The minimum documentation that Mrs Jones needs to be given at the first individual consultation meeting is: her individual score sheet, and the anonymised league table. Some employers might go the extra mile and also supply any supporting documentation that underpins the scores, for example absence records.

At the first individual consultation meeting Mrs Jones needs to be informed of how the scores were arrived at and who scored her. It is preferable if at least one of the employees who scored Mrs Jones is at the meeting, together with a representative from HR or someone who has responsibility for the HR function.

Explain that she will have the opportunity to give feedback at the second meeting on any issues she has with the scores awarded to her.

The second part of the individual consultation meeting is to share with the selected employee any vacancies the employer has or any associated employer. The employer should not assume that the employee will not be interested in any vacancy. No assumptions should be made about skill or experience as some selected employees may have experience or skills from other jobs that they are not displaying in their current role. For example, Mrs Jones before she took the job as a secretary may have been a fully qualified management accountant at a previous employer. Assumptions made about an employee's skills and experience can sometimes be incorrect.

The first consultation meeting should be for the employer to impart the documentation to support the selection and any alternative employment vacancies. The employer should be in transmit mode for the first meeting.

Where a redundancy is made during an employee's maternity leave, an employer has to comply with regulation 10 of MAPLE. Regulation 10 requires an employer to offer suitable available vacancies to the employee off on maternity leave. That employee gets priority on any vacancies.

The second meeting the employer should be in receive mode. The employee will be feeding back on the information and documentation received from the first meeting.

There are a host of variable outcomes from such a meeting, some of which could be:

1. Selection not agreed, some scores challenged. No interest in any alternative employment.

2. Selection not agreed. Scores challenged. Allegations of bias made.

3. Selection not agreed. Scores challenged. Allegations of discrimination made.

4. Selection agreed. Interest in one or more of any available vacancies.

5. Selection agreed. No interest in any alternative employment.

6. Selection agreed but the employee is on maternity leave and has the right under the maternity regulations to be offered any suitable available employment.

Because the employer has no advanced knowledge as to what points the employee will make at a second individual consultation meeting, the employer should go into such a meeting with an open mind. The employer should not go into the meeting with a redundancy confirmed, employment terminated letter. The redundancy can only be confirmed once consultation has concluded. The second meeting allows the employee to have his or her say.

Where the selection is not agreed, the employer should adjourn the meeting and go off and investigate the points raised and then feedback to the employee any findings and responses to the points raised at a re-convened meeting. That could be done on the day, it may take longer, particularly where allegations of bias or discrimination are made.

The employer will need to investigate, document the investigation, and come to a conclusion as to whether any of the points the employee has made have any merit. If the points raised do have merit and are sufficient to affect the scoring to such an extent that the employee is safe from redundancy then the employer will need to confirm that with the employee. Consultation should then start with the next employee in the league table.

Sometimes the points raised do have merit, result in an increase in scores, but the increase is insufficient to put the employee in a safe position in the league table. If that is the case that should be communicated to the employee. Employees are always happy to take any victory, even pyrrhic ones. However adjusted scoring does cast some doubt on the integrity and robustness of the original scoring process. A prudent employer would double check all the other scores to check that there are no other employees who need to have their scores adjusted.

When the adjourned meeting is reconvened make sure all points are answered. If all points have been answered then the employer can move on to confirming the selection and either progressing any interest shown in alternative employment or moving to termination.

If alternative employment is secured by the employee then there is no need for the employer to move to termination of employment. The employee can have a four-week trial period and decide whether to accept the new role or default back to having their employment terminated and leaving with a redundancy payment.

Only where the selection is agreed and there is no alternative employment or no interest in alternative employment can the employer close off the consultation process and confirm the selection. It is at that point termination of employment comes into view.

The key points about individual consultation are:

1. Share information.
2. Transmit as well as receive.
3. Investigate any points made.
4. If sufficient doubt over selection review selection and if necessary select someone else.
5. Be alive to rights of employees made redundant during maternity leave.

CHAPTER SEVEN

APPEALS AND GRIEVANCES

Once the individual consultation process is over, both employer and employee are at the crunch point – termination of employment. Because a termination of employment brings an employment to an end, many employers allow a right of appeal against termination. Those employers that don't have a right of appeal against redundancy dismissals may allow a grievance to be lodged by employees who have just had their contract terminated.

The ACAS Code of Practice on Discipline and Grievance does not apply to redundancy dismissals. So technically there is no legal right for an employee to be given a right of appeal when they are dismissed by reason of redundancy. The case law is well established.

An employer failing to give an employee a right of appeal in a redundancy dismissal will not have a sanction applied by an Employment Tribunal for breach of ACAS COP. There won't be a sanction applied as it won't amount to a breach of ACAS COP. Nor will a failure to give a right of appeal on its own make a dismissal unfair.

However, many employers will have an established redundancy procedure or process, where appeals are baked in as a right following a redundancy termination.

It makes sense to have a right of appeal. It is best practice to have a right of appeal. A right of appeal acts as a safety net for the employer to catch any defects in process. It makes perfect business sense to have such a safety net. Safety nets are a sensible precaution and act as a natural break between falling out of employment and landing up in Court.

So, if in doubt give employees a right of appeal. You would want a right of appeal in the same situation. Treat others as you would like to be treated. It makes sense.

However, before we get to a right of appeal, an employee has to have something to appeal about or be aggrieved about. That something is the termination of employment.

As we have seen earlier, leaving to one side the issues of constructive dismissal and expiry of a fixed term contract, the employment can be terminated in one of two ways.

Firstly, the employment can be terminated with notice of termination to expire on a given day. The employee could be required to work their notice or serve their notice at home on garden leave. The notice is almost always in writing. Having got this far in the process an employer would be unwise not to put a notice of termination in writing. Many contracts of employment require notice of termination to be in writing.

The written notice of termination should cover the following bases:

1. Reasons for redundancy.
2. Group consultation stage.
3. Selection.
4. Individual consultation meetings with dates.
5. The date notice starts and ends.
6. The right of appeal, including the date and method of lodging an appeal.
7. The redundancy payments and any other arrangements on termination, for example return of company property or pension arrangements.

There are a number of implications to an employee being given notice:

1. The employee has the statutory right to a reasonable amount of time off to look for work externally during the notice period. Reasonable is usually classed as two days per week.

2. If the employee's notice period is not at least a week longer than length of their statutory notice period i.e. a week for every year of service capped at twelve weeks, then if an employee is off sick during their notice period they are entitled to full pay during such a period of sickness. That right is enshrined in the Employment Rights Act 1996. That right has further been clarified in the case of Burlo v Langley a case involving an employment lawyer dismissing her nanny! The right does not apply where the notice period is a week or more longer than the statutory minimum. On a site closure where an employer may need to keep the factory running right up to the closure date, terminating employees' contracts with a notice period carries a substantial risk of the employees going off sick and being entitled to full pay during such sick leave.

3. Consultation will still be classed as ongoing during the notice period. Therefore, if alternative employment arises during the notice period then the employee should be told about such employment and be given an opportunity to consider and apply for it, if suitable.

4. Holiday will accrue up to the date notice expires.

5. Provided the contractual right exists, an employer may wish to require an employee to use up any accrued but untaken holiday during the notice period.

The road most taken by employers in a redundancy situation is to terminate the employee by giving them a payment in lieu of notice and ending their employment immediately. This reduces the operational risks outlined above. If the employer decides to dismiss with a payment in lieu then the letter should cover the following bases:

1. Reasons for redundancy.
2. Group consultation stage.
3. Selection.
4. Individual consultation meetings with dates.
5. The date employment ends.
6. The right of appeal, including the date and method of lodging an appeal.
7. The redundancy payments, the amount of payment in lieu and any other arrangements on termination, for example return of company property or pension arrangements. Any outplacement offered.

In law, a dismissal with a payment in lieu of notice amounts to a summary dismissal. A summary dismissal is a dismissal with immediate effect. The payment in lieu of notice amounts to a payment of damages where there is no reserved right to make a payment in lieu in the contract. Where there is a reserved right to make a payment in lieu then the payment in lieu amounts to the agreed way to terminate the contract.

The employees affected obviously will not be averse to receiving a lump sum for not doing any work. There is two slight wrinkles with paying in lieu of notice.

Firstly for those employees who have a restrictive covenant in their contract, a payment in lieu of notice is technically a breach of contract which may render the covenants unenforceable.

Following the De Geys case if the employer has no reserved right in the contract to make a payment in lieu of notice, then terminating the contract immediately without notice but with a payment in lieu will amount to a breach of contract. The employee has two choices to accept the breach and allow the contract to end or to affirm the breach and argue that the contract continues until terminated by notice or the PILON payment being paid.

It is obviously preferable to obtain employee buy in either during group consultation or individual consultation that that method of termination of employment has been agreed by the employee. If it has not been agreed there is a slight risk that termination of employment does not take place until a payment in lieu of notice has been paid.

In some cases the date employment terminates can have substantial consequences for example if LTIP awards vest or a bonus becomes due.

A payment in lieu of notice will be taxable. The tax on the payment has been complicated by recent legislation which classifies a payment in lieu of notice as Post-employment Notice Pay or PENP for short. There is a special calculation for PENPS and employers should consult up to date guidance on how PENPS should be taxed.

The other issue with a payment in lieu of notice is to make sure that the employee is no worse off financially than had he or she been given notice. If there is a reserved right in the contract for the employer to pay a payment in lieu, sometimes that contract stipulates how much the payment in lieu should be – for example basic pay only. Those cases are clear.

Less clear is what elements of variable pay to include in any calculation of payment in lieu. The key point is that the payment in lieu should not leave the employee worse off than had he or she been given notice unless the contract expressly provides for a calculation of a payment in lieu of notice for example basic pay only.

Holiday accrues to the date the employee leaves employment. Holiday does not accrue during the notional notice period.

Appeals and grievances

If the individual consultation has been conducted by the line manager who has made the selection some employees will not air their concerns. They don't air their concerns for a variety of reasons ranging from dislike of conflict, fear, ignorance and all points in between.

However, once the selection has been made and termination has been effected whether by notice or by payment in lieu of notice, sometimes selected employees see that they have little to lose and will table all their concerns by way of an appeal or a grievance.

An employer needs to hold an appeal meeting, investigate the points made, make findings on the points in issue and either uphold or reject the appeal. All the points that are made by the employee need to be determined. No fences should be sat on.

If the appeal is upheld then the question that needs to be asked and answered is whether the appeal points that are found in the employee's favour would have made any difference to the outcome. Would the employee still have been selected for redundancy notwithstanding? If so that needs to be stated in the outcome letter.

If the appeal points would have made a difference and the employee would not have been selected for redundancy then the employer has a choice:

1. Rescind the selection and offer to reinstate the employee to his or her former position. If the employee agrees to reinstatement, then re-instate with back pay and commence individual consultation with the next employee in the league table.

2. Rescind the selection and offer to reinstate the employee to his or her former position. If the employee does not agree to reinstatement and does not take the employer up on its offer, there are two consequences for the employee. It is arguable that upholding the appeal a failure to take up a reinstatement vanishes the earlier dismissal. The employee's failure to allow reinstatement will amount to a resignation not a dismissal. If it does not amount to a resignation and the employee remains dismissed then a failure to accept reinstatement will be a failure to mitigate losses, thereby potentially minimising any compensatory award if the employee goes to Employment Tribunal. An employee arguing for unfair dismissal when an employer has offered to reinstate the employee following a successful internal appeal does not have an attractive argument to make. An employment tribunal will not be immediately sympathetic to a complaint of unfair dismissal when the employee could have avoided the dismissal. Furthermore, the employer in upholding the appeal and offering to reinstate will have done everything a reasonable employer should have done.

3. Do not rescind the selection and enter into discussions with the employee about a settlement agreement. Obviously, the employer will not be in a strong bargaining position. However, if the employer has not communicated the outcome of the appeal or grievance to the employee then the employee may not realise how strong their bargaining position is. The employee may believe that their appeal has not succeeded and may be willing to accept a sum in compensation far smaller than an Employment Tribunal would award. Many employees are happy to be heard and come away from an appeal hearing believing that they have had a fair hearing. Listening without prejudice never did George Michael any harm, it won't do any harm for the manager hearing the appeal to listen in a concerned and attentive manner.

CHAPTER EIGHT

TAX AND SETTLEMENT AGREEMENTS

Employees who are made redundant often find the process difficult, particularly if the relationship with their employer is long standing and one based on mutual respect.

Most employers also find redundancy programmes hard work and disruptive, chopping the fat out of an organisation is an unpleasant and time-consuming experience. Very few employers relish redundancy exercises.

Most employers will want to move on quickly from a redundancy exercise which can be demotivating and demoralising for the remaining staff. Employers do not want to be discussing the redundancy exercise 12 or 24 months down the line at an Employment Tribunal. Redundancy exercises cause ripples in the market place and can lead to some employers being seen as trigger happy and not offering secure places of emplyment.

To mitigate these risks, legal and reputational, many employers opt to pay more than the legal minimum when making employees' redundant.

The legal minimum is:

1. Notice either served or paid in lieu.

2. Statutory redundancy payment.

A notice payment is taxable as Post-Employment Notice Pay or PENP. The formula for calculating PENP is not straightforward but should be built in to your payroll software.

However a statutory redundancy payment is tax free up to £30,000.00. All statutory redundancy payments are within the £30,000 tax free allowance on termination, leaving some of the tax free allowance unused.

Employers can and do make any additional payment over and above the Notice and Statutory Redundancy Payment. They do this to mitigate risk as well as generate some goodwill amongst departing employees. Some employers, perhaps the more hard-nosed ones, will offer a payment in lieu of notice rather than being served notice as a sweetener. The key difference not being the total amount received but the fact that a payment in lieu of notice payment is a one off lump sum payment, whereas if an employee is served notice then they receive their notice payments monthly for as long as the notice period which for senior employees could be 3 months, 6 months or 12 months. For those with long notice periods and large salary packages, a payment in lieu of notice can be the largest single item in a severance package.

Some employers make any additional payments conditional on signing a settlement agreement.

Practical Points

Many employers will mitigate the legal risks of claims by dismissed employees by offering settlement agreements.

The positives of offering settlement agreements are as follows:

1. Legal risks are mitigated, in particular the risk of legal claims.

2. Other risks are mitigated for example risks of reputational damage are reduced by clauses within the settlement agreement relation to disclosure of information and non-derogatory statements.

3. Other contractual rights are reinforced – for example the settlement agreement could refer to clauses in the contract of employment that impose post-termination obligation for example around confidential information or restrictive covenants.

4. Non-financial matters such as references and announcements are dealt with.

5. New contractual commitments can be entered into – for example if there are no restrictive covenants in the original contract of employment then they can be agreed in the settlement agreement.

6. It saves the time and expense of holding any appeals or grievance meetings.

7. It can close off any other outstanding issues such as subject access requests under the GDPR.

Negatives of entering into a settlement agreement:

1. Cost – the employer normally draws up the agreement or pays a Solicitor to draw up an agreement. The employer usually agrees to pay a contribution towards the employee's legal costs of taking advice on the settlement agreement.

2. The time cost in dealing with any queries the employee's solicitor may have.

3. The risk that the Solicitor may advise the employee to bring a legal claim as what is being offered in the agreement is less than the employee may win at Employment Tribunal. The employee may not otherwise have seen a Solicitor to take advice, had you, the employer, not offered a settlement agreement.

4. You don't get to test the procedure out. From an HR perspective the occasional claim in Employment Tribunal allows the employer to road test their procedure or process.

A settlement proposal could be:

1. Payment in lieu of 3 months' notice taxable at £12,000.00.

2. Statutory redundancy payment of £8,750.00 tax free.

3. A Termination Payment conditional on signing a settlement agreement of £5,000.00 tax free.

A settlement agreement has to be in a prescribed format as per section 203 of the Employment Rights Act 1996. The employee must receive advice on the implications of signing a settlement agreement from a prescribed person, usually a Solicitor or Trade Union Official with indemnity insurance.

Once a settlement agreement is signed the employee cannot bring any legal claims arising out of the termination of employment. The legal risk is mitigated.

Most settlement agreements also have non-derogatory statement clauses in to mitigate any reputational risk. An employer does not want employees they have made redundant bad mouthing them.

It is best to offer a settlement agreement towards the end of a redundancy exercise.

Employees sometimes instruct their Solicitor to negotiate the value of the agreement upwards, particularly if the extra payment is not that generous.

Employers put themselves in a good position in these negotiations by ensuring they have their ducks in a row. That means:

1. Robust evidence of consultation.

2. Robust evidence of a fair selection process.

Employers who offer settlement agreements too early in the redundancy process can sometimes find their negotiating position is weak as the employer cannot show robust evidence of a fair consultation and selection process as those processes may either be incomplete or not even started.

Once offered a settlement agreement, it is then difficult to put Humpty Dumpty together again if the negotiations do not end in agreement. Re-starting a redundancy process after failed negotiations is usually a recipe for an unhappy ending. The employer is then left making the redundancy which will look like a fait accompli.

If an employee is alleging pre-dismissal discrimination a sum in respect of injury to feelings can be included within the settlement as tax free over and above the £30,000 tax free allowance on termination payments. Tax free injury to feelings payments must be in connection with pre-dismissal alleged discrimination. What is and isn't pre-dismissal is not obvious but a discriminatory selection for redundancy could fall within the ambit for example selecting a pregnant woman for redundancy.

Injury to feelings awards are banded into lower, middle and upper band known as Vento bands. An employee's injury to feelings payment will ordinarily fall into the lower band unless the employee can show psychiatric harm caused by the discrimination. Employers can and do make payments equivalent to injury feelings awards in settlement agreements but those payments are usually limited to a lower band payment of between £5000 and £12,000.00. If you are concerned about making such a payment tax free over and above the tax free allowance on termination, prudent employers will seek HMRC clearance before payment.

An alternative to a settlement agreement is involving ACAS but that tends to be a more cumbersome process given ACAS's workload.

In summary towards the end of a redundancy process when selection has been confirmed many employers choose to offer a settlement agreement and more money to tie up all the loose ends in terms of residual risk.

CHAPTER NINE

CONCLUSIONS

This book has been a training exercise. As any trainer knows – you tell the audience what you are about to tell them, then you tell them, and then you tell them what you just told them.

This book does not give you a map. A map will give a number of definite routes to reach a destination. This book has given you a compass – by reading the compass you will know what direction you need to go in and what way you will need to be facing.

In particular I have set out a series of steps:

1. Proposal in writing, [**P**].

2. Group consultation with the affected employees or their appropriate representatives, [**G**].

3. Selection, [**S**].

4. Individual consultation with those selected, [**I**].

5. Termination and any appeals or grievances, [**T**].

So, where the organisation in which you work needs to make a redundancies the compass tells you to draw up a proposal – the first step, P. The proposal sets out the WRAPP:

1. **W**hat the organisation is planning to do – reduce the number of jobs.

2. **R**ationale for the reduction – cost cutting, introduction of technology, insert your particular reason.

3. A methodology for achieving the reduction – call for volunteers, pools, selection criteria, selection by interview.

4. Proposed timeline for achieving the reduction.

5. Proposed payments for those leaving as redundant.

The WRAPP mnemonic is full of Ps. As an HR Practitioner you have to mind your Ps. It is a plan and proposal, nothing is definite, nothing is decided. The WRAPP only becomes a decision after the second point has been completed.

The next step is G. G stands for Group Consultation.

Once the proposal is finalised the written proposal goes to those employees affected by the proposal or their appropriate representatives.

This I call the group consultation stage. It is agreeing a route with the employees or their representatives to achieve the reduction. Not only is it agreeing the route, it is also agreeing the need to take the journey.

Where there are fewer than twenty employees affected within a ninety-day period at one establishment, then the requirement to consult is less prescriptive.

If the proposal affects twenty or more employees at one establishment then the employer must consult with the appropriate representatives either the trade union or appropriate representatives of the employees elected for the purpose. The format for the WRAPP and the consultation process, including timelines, is more prescriptive where there are twenty or more employees affected. However, the mindset from the employer's perspective is the same.

The proposal goes to the affected employees or their appropriate representatives for their feedback and comment.

The proposal should be sufficiently detailed to allow for proper feedback. Furthermore, the proposal should be sufficiently detailed to allow employees in affected areas "to do the math." By that employees should have sufficient information to consider their own position and the probability that they will either be selected for redundancy or survive the cut.

Having the details on the pooling, proposed selection criteria and process for applying for voluntary redundancy sufficiently clear allows an organisation to give itself the best opportunity of achieving the reduction by voluntary means.

Allowing employees to volunteer for redundancy passes control to the employee but reduces the risk for confrontation. An application for voluntary redundancy is an alignment of the employer's and employee's interests. Win/win is always a result.

During the group consultation stage the employer is:

1. Reviewing any feedback on any aspect of the proposal.
2. Reverting back with points in response to the feedback.
3. If possible agreeing with the group, or their representatives, the following:
    a. The need for redundancies.
    b. The numbers of redundancies.
    c. The pools and selection processes.
    d. The timetable.
    e. The payment calculations for those who are made redundant.

Once the group consultation has been completed the organisation then makes the selections. The selection process is the next step – S.

Selection for redundancies should strive to achieve two purposes: firstly to leave the organisation fit for future purpose, secondly, to ensure that the employee selected for redundancy is the right employee. It is essential that the organisation uses the right tools for the job. Selection processes need to be adapted to suit the task at hand. If the task at hand is to remove costs because of pressing financial need, the selection criteria may be different to those used where the need for it is because of the introduction of new technology.

Once selections have been made the organisation moves on to the fourth step – individual consultation.

Individual consultation covers two issues:

1. The selection. The selected employee should be given a copy of the selection criteria, their scores and an anonymised league table.

2. Any alternative employment within the business or wider organisation or group business.

Once stage I is concluded you are at the end of the journey, T. The end of the journey can be at a terminus, here it is a termination of contract. The termination of contract can be with notice or without.

I hope you have enjoyed the book please feedback any comments to philip@pjhlaw.co.uk.

MORE BOOKS BY LAW BRIEF PUBLISHING

A selection of our other titles available now:-

'A Practical Guide to the Independent School Standards – September 2023 Edition' by Sarah McKimm
'A Practical Guide to Estate Administration and Crypto Assets' by Richard Marshall
'A Practical Guide to Managing GDPR Data Subject Access Requests – Second Edition' by Patrick O'Kane
'A Practical Guide to Parental Alienation in Private and Public Law Children Cases' by Sam King QC & Frankie Shama
'Contested Heritage – Removing Art from Land and Historic Buildings' by Richard Harwood QC, Catherine Dobson, David Sawtell
'The Limits of Separate Legal Personality: When Those Running a Company Can Be Held Personally Liable for Losses Caused to Third Parties Outside of the Company' by Dr Mike Wilkinson
'A Practical Guide to Transgender Law' by Robin Moira White & Nicola Newbegin
'A Practical Guide to 'Stranded Spouses' in Family Law' by Mani Singh Basi
'A Practical Guide to Residential Freehold Conveyancing' by Lorraine Richardson
'A Practical Guide to Pensions on Divorce for Lawyers' by Bryan Scant
'A Practical Guide to Challenging Sham Marriage Allegations in Immigration Law' by Priya Solanki
'A Practical Guide to Digital Communications Evidence in Criminal Law' by Sam Willis
'A Practical Guide to Legal Rights in Scotland' by Sarah-Jane Macdonald
'A Practical Guide to New Build Conveyancing' by Paul Sams & Rebecca East
'A Practical Guide to Defending Barristers in Disciplinary Cases' by Marc Beaumont
'A Practical Guide to Inherited Wealth on Divorce' by Hayley Trim
'A Practical Guide to Practice Direction 12J and Domestic Abuse in Private Law Children Proceedings' by Rebecca Cross & Malvika Jaganmohan

'A Practical Guide to Confiscation and Restraint' by Narita Bahra QC, John Carl Townsend, David Winch
'A Practical Guide to the Law of Forests in Scotland' by Philip Buchan
'A Practical Guide to Health and Medical Cases in Immigration Law' by Rebecca Chapman & Miranda Butler
'A Practical Guide to Bad Character Evidence for Criminal Practitioners by Aparna Rao
'A Practical Guide to Extradition Law post-Brexit' by Myles Grandison et al
'A Practical Guide to Hoarding and Mental Health for Housing Lawyers' by Rachel Coyle
'A Practical Guide to Psychiatric Claims in Personal Injury – 2nd Edition' by Liam Ryan
'Stephens on Contractual Indemnities' by Richard Stephens
'A Practical Guide to the EU Succession Regulation' by Richard Frimston
'A Practical Guide to Solicitor and Client Costs – 2nd Edition' by Robin Dunne
'Constructive Dismissal – Practice Pointers and Principles' by Benjimin Burgher
'A Practical Guide to Religion and Belief Discrimination Claims in the Workplace' by Kashif Ali
'A Practical Guide to the Law of Medical Treatment Decisions' by Ben Troke
'Fundamental Dishonesty and QOCS in Personal Injury Proceedings: Law and Practice' by Jake Rowley
'A Practical Guide to the Law in Relation to School Exclusions' by Charlotte Hadfield & Alice de Coverley
'A Practical Guide to Divorce for the Silver Separators' by Karin Walker
'The Right to be Forgotten – The Law and Practical Issues' by Melissa Stock
'A Practical Guide to Planning Law and Rights of Way in National Parks, the Broads and AONBs' by James Maurici QC, James Neill et al
'A Practical Guide to Election Law' by Tom Tabori
'A Practical Guide to the Law in Relation to Surrogacy' by Andrew Powell
'A Practical Guide to Claims Arising from Fatal Accidents – 2nd Edition' by James Patience
'A Practical Guide to the Ownership of Employee Inventions – From Entitlement to Compensation' by James Tumbridge & Ashley Roughton
'A Practical Guide to Asbestos Claims' by Jonathan Owen & Gareth McAloon

'A Practical Guide to Stamp Duty Land Tax in England and Northern Ireland' by Suzanne O'Hara
'A Practical Guide to the Law of Farming Partnerships' by Philip Whitcomb
'Covid-19, Homeworking and the Law – The Essential Guide to Employment and GDPR Issues' by Forbes Solicitors
'Covid-19 and Criminal Law – The Essential Guide' by Ramya Nagesh
'Covid-19 and Family Law in England and Wales – The Essential Guide' by Safda Mahmood
'A Practical Guide to the Law of Unlawful Eviction and Harassment – 2nd Edition' by Stephanie Lovegrove
'Covid-19, Brexit and the Law of Commercial Leases – The Essential Guide' by Mark Shelton
'A Practical Guide to Costs in Personal Injury Claims – 2nd Edition' by Matthew Hoe
'A Practical Guide to the General Data Protection Regulation (GDPR) – 2nd Edition' by Keith Markham
'Ellis on Credit Hire – Sixth Edition' by Aidan Ellis & Tim Kevan
'A Practical Guide to Working with Litigants in Person and McKenzie Friends in Family Cases' by Stuart Barlow
'Protecting Unregistered Brands: A Practical Guide to the Law of Passing Off' by Lorna Brazell
'A Practical Guide to Secondary Liability and Joint Enterprise Post-Jogee' by Joanne Cecil & James Mehigan
'A Practical Guide to the Pre-Action RTA Claims Protocol for Personal Injury Lawyers' by Antonia Ford
'A Practical Guide to Neighbour Disputes and the Law' by Alexander Walsh
'A Practical Guide to Forfeiture of Leases' by Mark Shelton
'A Practical Guide to Coercive Control for Legal Practitioners and Victims' by Rachel Horman
'A Practical Guide to the Law of Driverless Cars – Second Edition' by Alex Glassbrook, Emma Northey & Scarlett Milligan
'A Practical Guide to TOLATA Claims' by Greg Williams
'A Practical Guide to Elderly Law – 2nd Edition' by Justin Patten
'A Practical Guide to Responding to Housing Disrepair and Unfitness Claims' by Iain Wightwick

‘A Practical Guide to the Law of Bullying and Harassment in the Workplace’ by Philip Hyland

‘How to Be a Freelance Solicitor: A Practical Guide to the SRA-Regulated Freelance Solicitor Model’ by Paul Bennett

‘A Practical Guide to Prison Injury Claims’ by Malcolm Johnson

‘A Practical Guide to the Small Claims Track – 2nd Edition’ by Dominic Bright

‘A Practical Guide to Advising Clients at the Police Station’ by Colin Stephen McKeown-Beaumont

‘A Practical Guide to Antisocial Behaviour Injunctions’ by Iain Wightwick

‘Practical Mediation: A Guide for Mediators, Advocates, Advisers, Lawyers, and Students in Civil, Commercial, Business, Property, Workplace, and Employment Cases’ by Jonathan Dingle with John Sephton

‘The Mini-Pupillage Workbook’ by David Boyle

‘A Practical Guide to Crofting Law’ by Brian Inkster

‘A Practical Guide to the Law of Domain Names and Cybersquatting’ by Andrew Clemson

‘A Practical Guide to the Law of Gender Pay Gap Reporting’ by Harini Iyengar

‘NHS Whistleblowing and the Law’ by Joseph England

‘Employment Law and the Gig Economy’ by Nigel Mackay & Annie Powell

‘A Practical Guide to Noise Induced Hearing Loss (NIHL) Claims’ by Andrew Mckie, Ian Skeate, Gareth McAloon

‘An Introduction to Beauty Negligence Claims – A Practical Guide for the Personal Injury Practitioner’ by Greg Almond

‘Intercompany Agreements for Transfer Pricing Compliance’ by Paul Sutton

‘Zen and the Art of Mediation’ by Martin Plowman

‘A Practical Guide to the SRA Principles, Individual and Law Firm Codes of Conduct 2019 – What Every Law Firm Needs to Know’ by Paul Bennett

‘A Practical Guide to Adoption for Family Lawyers’ by Graham Pegg

‘A Practical Guide to Industrial Disease Claims’ by Andrew Mckie & Ian Skeate

‘A Practical Guide to Conducting a Sheriff Court Proof’ by Andrew Stevenson

‘A Practical Guide to Vicarious Liability’ by Mariel Irvine

‘A Practical Guide to Applications for Landlord’s Consent and Variation of Leases’ by Mark Shelton

‘A Practical Guide to Relief from Sanctions Post-Mitchell and Denton’ by Peter Causton

'A Practical Guide to Equity Release for Advisors' by Paul Sams
'A Practical Guide to Financial Services Claims' by Chris Hegarty
'The Law of Houses in Multiple Occupation: A Practical Guide to HMO Proceedings' by Julian Hunt
'Occupiers, Highways and Defective Premises Claims: A Practical Guide Post-Jackson – 2nd Edition' by Andrew Mckie
'A Practical Guide to Financial Ombudsman Service Claims' by Adam Temple & Robert Scrivenor
'A Practical Guide to Running Housing Disrepair and Cavity Wall Claims: 2nd Edition' by Andrew Mckie & Ian Skeate
'A Practical Guide to Holiday Sickness Claims – 2nd Edition' by Andrew Mckie & Ian Skeate
'Arguments and Tactics for Personal Injury and Clinical Negligence Claims' by Dorian Williams
'A Practical Guide to Drone Law' by Rufus Ballaster, Andrew Firman, Eleanor Clot
'A Practical Guide to Compliance for Personal Injury Firms Working With Claims Management Companies' by Paul Bennett
'RTA Allegations of Fraud in a Post-Jackson Era: The Handbook – 2nd Edition' by Andrew Mckie
'RTA Personal Injury Claims: A Practical Guide Post-Jackson' by Andrew Mckie
'On Experts: CPR35 for Lawyers and Experts' by David Boyle
'An Introduction to Personal Injury Law' by David Boyle

These books and more are available to order online direct from the publisher at www.lawbriefpublishing.com, where you can also read free sample chapters. For any queries, contact us on 0844 587 2383 or mail@lawbriefpublishing.com.

Our books are also usually in stock at www.amazon.co.uk with free next day delivery for Prime members, and at good legal bookshops such as Wildy & Sons.

We are regularly launching new books in our series of practical day-to-day practitioners' guides. Visit our website and join our free newsletter to be kept informed and to receive special offers, free chapters, etc.

You can also follow us on Twitter at www.twitter.com/lawbriefpub.

www.ingramcontent.com/pod-product-compliance
Lightning Source LLC
LaVergne TN
LVHW022056200926
848481LV00003B/940
9781916698291